Online Marketing for the Modern Small to Mid-Size Business

ITTS | INTEGRATED TOTAL
TECHNOLOGY SOLUTIONS

Ivan Jackson Jr

with

Ryan Healy

This publication is designed to provide accurate and authoritative information in regard to the subject matter covered. It is sold with the understanding that the publisher is not engaged in rendering legal, accounting or other professional service. If legal advice or other expert assistance is required, the services of a competent professional person should be sought.

The author of this publication has made his best effort to provide accurate and up to date information, but is in no way responsible for any changes in information from the time of publication, or from any inaccuracies within the text.

This publication makes no guarantees or warrantees of any kind regarding the success of the techniques provided within as the individual use of the information is critical to potential success. This publication is for informational purposes only and the author is clear of any and all liability relating to the information provided within. The author is not responsible for any damages or consequences resulting from the action or inaction taken by the user based on the information provided in this publication. All names of people, institutions or businesses are fictional.

Alteration, reproduction or redistribution of this product in whole or in part without the express written permission of the author is forbidden and illegal. You do not have permission to share, sell, trade or distribute this publication in any way. This publication may be watermarked electronically.

By using this publication, the user agrees that they have read this disclaimer in full and accepts these terms in full.

Contents

Section One

Why Your Business Needs The Web

Introduction

Welcome to *Online Marketing for the Modern Small to Mid-Size Business*. If you're reading this, it probably means you're either a business owner or the manager of a business, and that you're interested in learning more about how you can take advantage of the many benefits that utilizing the internet for marketing can provide to your business. Whether you're currently already using the web to some extent, but want to do more, or you're not on the web at all, you've come to the right place.

By the end of reading this you'll have a deeper understanding of not only *why* it is so important that your business be using the internet as optimally as possible, but also *how* you can utilize the tools available online to the benefit of your business. You'll learn the different areas of internet marketing and the techniques that can be employed within each of those areas.

You'll learn the options you have for getting your business online in the best way possible to meet the goals of your business, to reflect the professionalism and quality of your business and it's products or services, and more importantly, to be profitable and worthwhile as a whole. Because make no mistake, being on the web just for the sake of it, and doing it wrong, is far from profitable, in fact, it can be costly. So it needs to be done right. That means everything from choosing which type of site is best for your business, to branding that site, and ensuring that your site is as easy as possible for users to find on the net.

In section two, you'll learn the keys to using your company's web presence to reach out onto the web to expose your business to your target markets and to bring in new clients. This includes the best ways to target your company's advertising, reaching out to local consumers in order to maximize the return you get from your web marketing efforts, collecting important information on potential clients for use later in your sales cycle, optimizing your campaigns for the best possible conversion, and much more.

Section three will cover one of the most important things that being on the web can do for your business, which is give you a powerful, efficient, and easy way to keep in close contact with your existing clients as well as with new customers. Keeping in constant contact is one of the most important steps in ensuring a strong relationship with customers and clients, and an absolute key to ensuring repeat business. You'll learn about the tools that you can employ to keep your clients up to date and in the loop on everything to do with your business, including methods like using auto-responders, writing business blogs, and using the ever popular social media outlets that are taking over the internet.

In short, when you close this book after reading the last page, you'll have a complete picture of the world of marketing on the web. What this book is *not* is a technical manual. Don't expect to be an computer programmer or graphic designer when you're finished. But what you will be is highly knowledgeable on the ins and outs of web marketing, and you'll be able to make informed, well directed decisions about the ways that you company can and should use the web as an integral part of its marketing mix in order to increase sales and maximize profits.

Modern Marketing

There is a very big problem that marketers and businesses face in today's world. This is a problem that marketers of old did not have to face, or at least faced much less. That problem is that consumers today are incredibly good at *ignoring* marketing messages. It used to be you could just plaster up your signs or run your ad spot, and you'd get through to people with reasonable success. Today though, people just tune out. We are so inundated by marketing messages, every day of our lives, that we've become incredibly adept at simply turning a blind eye to them. After all, if we actually paid attention to each and every marketing message thrown our way each day, we wouldn't have time to eat or sleep.

Consumers today are exposed to between 3,500 and 5000 marketing messages per day compared to just 500 to 2,000 messages per day in the '70's[1]. That's an absolutely huge increase and the odds are, those numbers are probably only going to keep rising. Big corporations have money to burn and if anyone thinks the likes of Coca-Cola, Apple, et al are going to stop hitting us with ads every chance they get, it's time to think again.

So what do you do then if you aren't a Fortune 500 company and you don't have eleventy-billion dollars[2]? Well the answer is that you have to make the marketing messages you do put out there count for more, and you need to do it in a couple of key areas. The first area is in the effectiveness of those messages in getting through the ad blindness and actually reaching the target. The second way is through cost effectiveness. You need to make every dollar you spend on marketing and advertising count for more. With the number of marketing messages that get ignored on a day to day basis, you can't afford to spend a single penny on being just another member of the blur.

Engaging Your Customers

So how do you go about making your messages more effective at reaching people and ensuring that they don't just shut you out like they are almost every other promotional message thrown their way?

---

[1] According to J. Walker Smith, president of consumer and marketing watcher Yankelovich

[2] If you don't get this reference, search 'Keanu Reeves Celebrity Jeopardy' in Google!

Simple, you engage them. Well, ok, maybe simple isn't the best word to use, because in reality, it's simple in concept and theory, but not so much so in practical application. After all, a lot of very big companies, with very big budgets, make very big mistakes with it and end up with very big flops that cost them very big piles of cash. So let's talk about engagement for a second.

Engagement basically means that rather than marketing *at* your target customers, you need to market *with* them. Remember, the days of just beaming out a thousand messages to your target market and having them run in to your business to give you all their money are gone, long gone. So you need to stop thinking about your target market as a pile of money that could be yours if you just drive your ads into their brains hard enough, and more like your little kid. Wait, what? 'Like my little kid?' you're saying. Yes, exactly, and here's why.

Little kids are almost exactly like consumers in one very important way. Little kids are incredibly good at completely ignoring things they aren't interested in. Try bringing a six year old to the opera or your book club and see how long they pay attention for. It'll probably be somewhere between zero and three seconds. Unless you give them something they want to pay attention to, they will not, nay, they *cannot* spare even a shred of attention. So what do you do? You give them what they want. You bring them to the opera *with* a comic book. You bring them to your book club *with* their Game Boy.

Your target market is no different. No, I'm not saying you should buy them all Game Boys or comic books, but you *should* give them what they want. You need to engage them on their terms, in a way that will make them *want* to pay attention to what you have to say, and unless you do, you will just be one more billboard among a million others that they're ignoring.

This isn't necessarily easy, and it often takes some creativity, but there are plenty of ways to do it. How you engage your potential client or customer really depends completely on what your market is and who your targets are. Beer companies, for instance, engage their primary targets (young males) by making funny, and highly memorable ads that feature ridiculous premises (in fact, if you look closely you'll see the trend towards funny commercials is rapidly growing). How you do it will depend on who you're marketing to and how they *want* to be marketed to. Luckily for you, the internet gives you a ton of ways to find out this particular information, and a ton of ways to actually deliver your messages in ways that people *want* to be marketed to.

Cost Effective Marketing

Now how about that cost effective marketing bit? Well, let's face the facts, most businesses, more than likely yours included, don't have the seemingly unlimited budgets that some gigantic corporations do, and so just pouring wheelbarrow after wheelbarrow of money into

marketing efforts is probably out of the question. Every single dollar spent on marketing has to be making a difference. Unfortunately, for most traditional marketing channels, that's not so easy to do.

We've all heard that old expression, "I know half of my marketing works, I just don't know which half." Well, that statement is almost painfully true. That is, if you're one of the companies lucky enough to have half of your marketing working! The reality is, even if half of your marketing is doing a great job, the other half is draining money from you, so wouldn't it be nice if you could identify it and either sever it from your marketing mix, or tweak and adjust it to be more effective?

That is the key to cost effective marketing. Knowing *exactly* what is working and what isn't. When you know what doesn't work, you know exactly what needs to be changed. When you know what does work, you know exactly what you should be doing more of. But when you're not sure, then you know almost nothing, and you're swinging in the dark. Unfortunately, for a great deal of companies, this is how their marketing operates. They're putting in the time and money, and they're doing their research, and they're seeing some results, but they don't actually know exactly where those results are coming from, how much better or worse those results could be with changes to their marketing campaigns, and where those changes should be made if they turn out to be necessary.

Think about it, you spend thousands of dollars every month on a nice full color ¼ page ad in the local Yellow Pages. It's got a nice description of your business and you've got a great photo of your staff. You know it looks great, you know you love it, but what don't you know? Well, first and most importantly, you probably don't really know how many new clients it brings you. You know you're getting new business every month, and you *think* it probably comes from that ad, and you might even give your customers a "how did you find us?" survey. But the odds are, if you're anything like the vast majority of businesses, you don't know the exact percentage of new customers, or the exact dollar value in new business, that are being generated by that Yellow Pages advertisement.

You also don't know if your ad is performing to its full potential or not. It looks good, sure, but does it perform as good as it could be? What if you changed the headline? What if you used a photo of your product instead of your staff? What if you changed the font? Seems like frivolous stuff right? Well it isn't. In fact it's extremely important and can make huge differences in how that ad performs, and how much value you get out of the thousands of dollars you spend on it every month. Unfortunately, it's almost impossible, or at least a huge pain in the butt, for you to test this and therefore highly unlikely you'll ever really be sure if the 5 new clients the ad provides each month could actually be 10 of 15.

This same principal applies across most marketing channels, especially the ones commonly used by small and medium sized businesses. Marketing is all about getting the best success rate possible from each ad or marketing message you put out. But without knowing these key metrics, you're really in the dark about how well your campaigns are performing, and in turn, how the dollars you spend on those campaigns are performing.

Where the Internet Comes In

S o where does the internet play into all of this? Why is it *so* important for businesses to be not only using the web, but using it as a major part of their marketing mix? What makes the net so special over all the other ways that a business can market itself to existing and potential clients? Well, there are a few parts to that answer, but what it comes down to is that the net is 1) where your customers are, 2) the easiest and cheapest place to access your customers, 3) somewhere your customers *want you to be*, and 4) somewhere you can get all the information on what those customers want, need, are doing, aren't doing, think of your product, think of you, think of your suit, think of your hat, and just about everything else you could ever want to know.

Where Your Customers Are

Let's talk about some very important numbers. One of which might be the most important number in this entire book. First, here's a really big one; as of December 2008, there were over one billion internet users worldwide[3]. One billion! And that number is only going to get larger and larger. After all, there are over six billion people on earth and each day more and more become web savvy! But still, who cares about worldwide usage right? After all, the odds are you're probably not too concerned with selling your product or service halfway around the globe. Maybe you are, or maybe you will, but for the sake of argument, let's say you're like the average business, and you're not.

So let's look a little more locally, a perfect opportunity to present your second set of numbers. If you're reading this, the odds are you live in North America or Europe. If you're in North America, then you have over 185 million internet users[4] within the borders of your continent. If you're in Europe, that number is even higher, at almost 283 million users[5]. We could keep whittling these numbers down further and further and further until we're studying the number of internet users in your bathroom, but there isn't any need because I'm sure you get the point. There are a *ton* of people on the internet, and these gigantic numbers filter right down into *your* local area. If you're

---

[3] According to comScore, the leader in worldwide web usage statistics.

[4] Ibid

doing business in a town or city in North America or Europe, the odds are, the majority of people you're selling to locally are also online.

Now let's look at a couple more important numbers. According to studies, 81% of American internet users have said they've used the internet to research a product they were planning to buy, with 20% saying they do online purchase research on an average day. In addition, 66% said they've purchased something online.[6] These are hugely important statistics for obvious reasons. People are buying online, a lot of them, and even more are using the web to research purchases they plan to make whether it be online or in a real brick and mortar (B&M) setting. These are your customers; regardless of what it is you're selling.

It's a simple fact of life that people today love to use the net to research things they're planning on spending money on, and this goes for both consumers and for B2B. So if you sell a product or service that people are going to want to research before buying, which means basically anything that costs more than pocket change, you'd be crazy not to give them their a way to do it. Remember what we said earlier about marketing to your prospects where they *want* to be marketed to? This is an example of just that.

---

[5] Ibid

[6] According to statistics from Pew Research.

You simply can't ignore the fact that the very people you're trying to sell to, whether they be a kid, a mom, or the buyer for a major corporation, are almost certain on the net (especially if you're selling to the ever profitable 18-35 male demographic, in which chase they actually *live* on the internet.)

Now let's look at the final number I'm going to throw at you in this section, and this one is the most important one, as I said earlier, maybe the important number in this entire book! That ever important stat is that search engines currently account for 31% of all local business searches done[7]. Print yellow pages account for 30%. This is of huge significance. What this means is that the yellow pages has been bumped off as the number one source for local business information. If you were to include online local directories, the number of people going offline rather than turning to the big yellow book is even higher. Couple those numbers with the fact that yellow pages use goes down by about 3% every year, and the writing is on the wall. The fact of the matter is, the internet is now the place where most people prefer to go to find local businesses.

So we know the web is where people go to find local businesses, and we know the web is where people go to research products and services they plan to purchase, so, if you're *not* on the web, or are, but half-heartedly, then what does that mean? Well, what

---

[7] According to a comScore study commissioned by TMP Directional Marketing

it means is that you're losing business every single day to your competitors that *are* utilizing the web for all its worth. Those competitors are the ones coming up at the top of the search engines when people go looking for a product or service, they're the ones giving people everything they want to know about those products and services, they're the ones who building trust with clients that could potentially be yours, and last but not least, they're the ones bringing in those sales, and enjoying those profits. In short, you literally cannot afford to ignore the web. Ignoring the web is ignoring your customer base and if you're guilty of it in any way, then you're leaving money on the table.

The Web Is a Marketers Dream

So now we know that your customers are hanging out on the web, and that you really need to be concentrating on meeting them there, but not only should you be, but you should *want* to be, because the web is probably the single greatest place on Earth when it comes to marketing. We talked earlier about how important it is to engage your customers in ways they want to be engaged, and to get the most out of your marketing dollars, and it just so happens that the internet is the perfect place to do both of these things.

The internet is the perfect place to engage your customers with marketing messages because you have four great ways of reaching them that are unobtrusive and enjoyable for them (and a couple that are a little more in your face, too). First of all, you have search engines and local business listings. These are your bread and butter on the web because when people find your business through a search engine or local listing, you know that they're probably looking specifically for what it is that you sell or do. You're not hitting them with some marketing message they don't want to hear, they're actually seeking you out. They want what you have, and you're glad to give it to them.

You've got to be seen though. Because if instead of you they find your competitor, or his site is far more informative than yours, then you're screwed. You can do this either be being at the tops of the organic searches and local directories, or another option you have for this is contextual advertising. Contextual advertising shows your ad (normally a small text ad or banner) when someone searches for a term relating to your product or service. So if someone types in "car floor mats" or "Toledo legal services" in Google, you can pay to have your ad show up alongside the search listings.

You also have a ton of other ways to engage your potential customers and clients on the net, most of which focus on being there with your marketing messages when your potential customers *want* to see them. This includes participating in online communities, using social media, providing valuable content (whether that means enjoyable entertainment, highly useful information or something else), and more. The key is that you won't just be forcing your marketing messages on your target audience, because as we discussed earlier, that just doesn't work at all.

How about that cost effectiveness thing? Well that is probably one of the places where the web really stands out the most. Advertising and marketing on the web are incredibly cheap. Whether you're trying to do market research or trying to sell your latest widget, doing so on the web will almost always be significantly cheaper than doing so through offline mediums. Whether it be supplementing or shedding your insanely expensive yellow pages ad in favor of an effective, professional website, or spending just a few cents per click to get potential customers to your offer, things on the web just tend to be more cost effective.

However, this low cost of advertising isn't even where the real value in marketing on the web lies. It's important, yes, but it's only at the surface. The real value relates to the measurability issue we touched on earlier. Remember that old adage we mentioned, "I know half of my marketing works, but not which half"? Well toss that right out the window, because with the web, you *do* know which half. In fact, the degree of analysis that the web provides you with is almost overwhelming, and you can narrow down information from your marketing campaigns to such an amazing level that you can literally track success down to individual visitors should you want to.

So now, rather than know *something* within your marketing mix is working, you know exactly what is working. But more importantly, you know exactly what isn't working. You can then test and tweak those underperforming campaigns until they do work. Doing this you can systematically work through your marketing until everything that doesn't work is gone and all that is left are the methods and techniques that produce the best results.

This is where the internet is your best friend. Marketing on the web, through careful (and thorough) testing, you can eliminate all those bad marketing dollars that weren't bringing you results. That money stays in your pocket, and the money you do spend works harder for you, producing better results and generating more revenues and more profits. There is no offline marketing medium that gives you that kind of control and that kind of measurability. Only the web provides insight to that depth, and businesses that don't make use of that huge advantage are missing out big time.

So now you know all about the *why*, now it's time to start looking at the *how*. Section two will teach you about getting your business up and running on the web.

Section Two

Getting Your Business on the Web

Business Websites

It's no coincidence that every major corporation has a website for each of their major brands, and in many cases even unique sites for individual product lines. Your website is your face on the internet and without one you have no representation on the web. When you meet a potential client, or chat with an existing one in real life, you, or your employees, are the face of your business. They represent your business, what it stands for and the quality of your products and services. This is exactly the function that your website serves on the internet. It is your online ambassador between your business and your customers.

So what kind of functions do business websites perform? Well, first it's important to note that not all business websites are alike, and quite often there simply isn't one fit-all solution for all things marketing. Your business website might be a simple "business card" style site, which is basically just a simple site with only a few pages that is intended solely to give you a presence on the web so that potential customers can get vital information like your location, your contact information or your business hours.

Or your site might be designed as an e-commerce site where you sell your physical products, giving potential customers both locally and on a larger scale the ability to purchase from you right on your website and have their orders shipped to their homes. You could also use your site as a lead capture system to move potential clients into and through your sales funnel. You could use your site to collect data on potential and existing customers in order to use in later marketing campaigns. Or your site could be an online catalogue providing detailed information on your products or services for the many web users who do their purchase research online.

The point is, there are many things a business site can do. It's amazing that a website is so much more versatile and so much more functional than any yellow pages ad or print ad, and yet so many businesses completely ignore them, either not having one, or having a poor one that they let go under-utilized. In the following chapters, we'll go through the nuts and bolts of what you need to consider in order to make sure your company's website is doing all that it can be doing for your business.

The Importance of Quality

B efore going any further, it's incredibly important that we first talk about quality and the incredibly importance that quality and professionalism have to your website. Like we said earlier, your website is your face on the web. It represents who you and your business are and what you and your business stand for. Get it right, and it will be an invaluable asset that will bring in many, many times its cost in profits. But get it wrong, and it will actually cost you business.

Yep, that's right, a poorly done website can actually cost you business. That's because if an internet user doesn't find you on the net, they may never know you exist, but it won't prejudice them against doing business with you in the future. But if an internet user lands on your website, and it's amateurish and unprofessional, it will leave a negative impression with them that very well *could* cost you business in the future. So it's important to get your website right. You wouldn't put anything but your best face forward towards a client in real life, and the exact same should go for the web.

So what is quality? Well, let's talk about what quality isn't. We've all been to those websites that look like they were designed in 1996 and are bright green with red text and spinning images in the corners. We've also all been to websites with links that don't work, spelling mistakes, childish fonts, etc. Do these scream "trust worthy" to you? No. What they show is that the businesses running them can't be bothered to pay attention to details, even such major ones. What does that say about the business? It says that they'll treat clients the exact same way. I'll say it again; remember that your website is a representation of your company.

That's the key when it comes to quality. If you look at the site and you say, "meh, it's alright I guess", then it isn't alright. Would you deliver a product or service to a client and say "meh, it's good enough"? No way. Would you be satisfied with a "decent" performance during a presentation to a prospective customer? No way. So why do so many businesses settle for amateurish websites? Don't be part of that group. And it is a big group. Now that doesn't mean your site has to be designed by Michelangelo and make visitors cry when they see its beauty. It just means that you should take the same pride in your website that you take in every other aspect of your business. It can be very easy to let your website go because unlike your appearance, or your office, or your face to face interactions with clients, it's digital and doesn't really exist in the real world. You wouldn't wear a dirty suit, it'd bug you all day, but don't stop by your website for a while and you may quickly forget that it could use a polishing.

Luckily, any professional website designer worth their weight will understand this and make sure they do a good job of giving you a website that is deserving of being associated with your business. But for the love of everything good, use a website designer. It doesn't matter how tempted you are or how easy someone told you it is, don't try to do it yourself unless you're an expert. And don't think that you can just hire the neighbors' kid to do it. Remember, just any old website is worthless, and a bad one might actually harm your business. So if you have a website, take another look! Go and spend some time really looking over it. Anything you see that could be better? And if you don't have one yet and you're going to get one done, make sure it's being done by someone who understands its importance and can provide you with something excellent enough to attach your company's name to.

Website Quality: Don't Accept Just Anything!

Which of these two websites would give you a better first impression? Design quality matters!

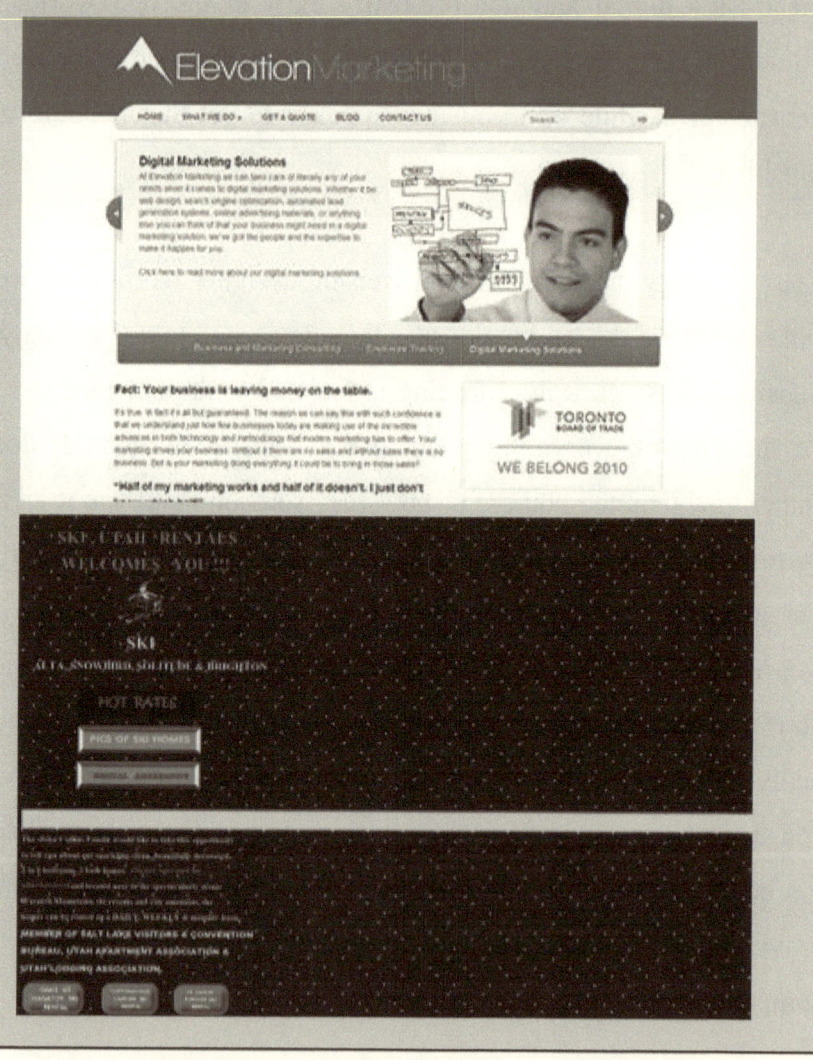

Domain Names

D omain names are literally the addresses of the web. When someone needs to mail you something, they send it to your physical address. When someone wants to go to your website, they'll type in your web address. The difference between a web address and a real address though is that your physical address probably isn't part of your branding, and the odds are you don't have a specific house and street number you want to use, that may very well already be taken by someone else! Welcome to the world of domain names!

Your domain name is part of your branding. You want people to be able to remember what your website is if possible, and ideally you *should* own your businesses own name as a domain.

Unfortunately, that can be difficult since most dot-com domain names are already taken up. This is especially true if your business operates under a name that is fairly common overall. You might be the only Smith Inc. in your area, but that doesn't mean that Smith.com is going to be available (it isn't, in case you were inclined to check!) So what do you do if yourbusinessname.com is unavailable? Well you have some options.

First, you can look to other extensions. Dot-net is a popular alternative, or, if you can use your countries top-level-domain, i.e. .co.uk for Britain, .ca for Canada, etc. Often times names that are unavailable as dot-com will be up for grabs in these extensions. Secondly, you can look to add descriptive words into your domain name. For instance if your business name is Apex, and you're an automotive brake manufacturer, when you can't get Apex.com, you can always try ApexAutomotive.com, ApexBreaks.com, etc. As long as the domain isn't so long it's impossible to remember, or totally unrelated to your business, it'll be ok. But your domain ideally should have your business name in it somewhere at the very least.

There is also another domain option that any business that operates locally should explore, even those that already have their business name as a domain. That option is domains based around local keywords. The reason these domains are worthwhile is that when a potential customer does a search in Google, the domain name is factored into the algorithm that decides which entries to show first. So for example, if a web user goes to Google and types in "Cincinnati Orthopedic Surgeons", then the website with the domain name CincinnatiOrthopedicSurgeon.com will get a boost in the search rankings and will likely come up prominently.

Many of these keyword rich, location specific domain names are readily available, and businesses that operate locally should always consider them for their web marketing efforts. The best way to use such domains is to register your main domain which will ideally be your business name, and then use local keyword domains to redirect to that site. For instance, a computer store named Mitchell Computers operating in Toronto, Ontario could register MitchellComputers.com (or .ca) as their main site domain, and then also register TorontoComputerStore.com and TorontoComputerSales.com to use as redirect sites or clone sites.

One important question that often comes up is what to do if a company's name.com isn't available, but is up for sale. How much is a domain worth and at what price is it worth it to buy? Well, that is a pretty tough question to answer because what it comes down to is that the answer is different for each company depending on their unique situation. For instance, a company that sells industrial equipment and does millions of dollars in business every year should not hesitate to spend thousands of dollars to have their own business name as their domain name. However, a small mom and pop store who is branching out on to the web likely won't be able to spend big bucks to get their domain name, and realistically, it probably isn't even that important to them.

One thing is for absolute certain though, domain names are going, and they're going fast. Most short dot-com domains and most dot-com domains with common words are already gone, and many of the other extensions are quickly beginning to sell out. So if you don't already have your domain name, you should probably seriously considering hitting the web and seeing what's available, because if you wait too long, you might miss out on everything good and end up having to spend some serious cash in order to secure yourself a quality domain name for your businesses web efforts.

Setting Goals for Your Website

The most important step you can take in the early development stages of getting your company's website built and up and running online is to set clear goals for what you want the website to accomplish both now and in the future. A website that is just thrown up without direction, assuming it's designed well, is still better than nothing, but you can't truly reap the full benefits of being on the web unless your marketing efforts have direction, and setting clear, precise, measurable goals for your site is the first step in doing so. The importance lies in the fact that not every site is going to be able to accomplish every goal, and you may need to design and build certain sections of your site differently in order for them to perform and meet the goals you set out. So let's go over a few of the common goals that businesses can set for their websites, the technical aspects of which will be discussed later on in the book.

Online Business Card

The online business card site is probably the least complicated type of site that a business can put up. Simply put, the goal is to provide the vital information of a business, such as their name, location, business hours, phone number, email address, and the like. These kinds of sites are often the starting points for companies just getting on the web because they don't take much to plan, don't take much to set up, and they do serve a very important purpose, namely giving web users somewhere to land that will provide them with more information about your business, albeit in slim amounts.

If you do decide to put up an online business card style site, remember that even though it's simple, it still has a purpose and it still needs to move the visitor into another action. You put your phone number on the site so the visitor has the option to call you, you put your email address on the site so they can email you, etc. So whatever you do, do not leave out any piece of contact information whatsoever. Since the site itself doesn't perform any real sales function, you have to be absolutely sure that the visitor is alerted to every single option they have in getting hold of you so that hopefully, they will eventually make a purchase. Here is a list of things that you should have on your business card style site;

- Your company name and company logo.
- Your company address (whether that be the address of your office, your retail outlet[s], etc. Anywhere you want potential clients to be able to go should be included.)
- All telephone numbers applicable to clients. If you do business locally only this might just be your local number. If you do business on a larger scale, consider getting a toll free number.
- At least one email address, but preferably more. Ideally you should have an email for customer service, an email for sales inquiries, one for billing, one for tech. support [if applicable]. You can forward them all to the same catch-all address if you want, but people like to see "departments", even if they don't really exist.
- Business hours for all locations listed.
- A map! This is an important one. Don't make clients go off-site to find directions to the address you list on your site. Include a map so they can see exactly where you are. You can install an interactive map powered by Google on your site for free.
- A call to action! Now the visitor knows who you are, where you are, when you're open, how to call you, and how to email you. Now *ask* them to. Use a strong call to

action to get them to use that information and pick up the phone or jump in the car.

One word of warning about business card style sites though; they leave a *lot* on the table. Yes, you're on the web, and it's definitely a good start. It's good you're providing that information to prospective customers, but there is so much more you could be doing. What if that customer leaves your site and never comes back? What if they want to buy immediately? What if they need information on your services but it's after business hours? There is so much more you could be doing with your site, so think bigger!

Informational / Catalogue Style

Regardless of whether or not your company sells tangible products or intangible services, you can benefit greatly from having a more in depth, information filled site explaining in detail exactly what it is that you do or sell. As opposed to a simple business card site, this site will generally contain quite a few more pages, and quite a bit more information. It will still have all of the important information that a business card style site will have, but the goal of this type of site is to give your site visitor all the information they need on your products or services.

Catalogue sites are perfect for companies that sell products or services that require a degree of research on the part of the buyer, but might not be the best choice for businesses that provide products or services that don't require as much thought from the purchaser. For instance, a business selling specialized office equipment will definitely want to have a solid amount of information listed on their web site so that potential buyers can research their products easily. However, a plumbing service probably won't benefit much from having a website packed full of information. A website is definitely something that plumbing business should have, but let's be realistic, when someone goes to Google to find a local plumber for an emergency off-hours repair, they probably don't need to browse through too much information to know that this is the right guy to fix their broken toilet.

That's the key with websites. You need to include all of the necessary information that your customers are looking for, but you don't want to over-crowd your site with unnecessary information. Too much information could overwhelm people and actually end up forcing them off of your site! Remember, if people are looking for more information, then they'll be happy it's there, but if they don't want information, then they'll be annoyed if they have to sift through a ton of text to find what they *are* looking for. For instance, when someone visits that local plumber's site, if they have to dig through a history of plumbing and a technical description of drainage system in order to find the phone number, they'll probably be heading for another plumbers site pretty quickly.

One very effective way to do a catalogue site is to provide both short length descriptions and full descriptions of your products or services. Keep your home page clean and clutter free, and link to seeded inner pages with the descriptions of your products or services. On your main product page, for each product provide short descriptions and a link to read more which then takes the visitor to a detailed page dedicated to that particular product with a full description.

E-Commerce Sites

E-commerce sites are websites that are designed to allow the visitor to purchase directly from the site without having to visit the store or business to make the transaction. Depending on your business and your product or service, this can be a very good way to increase sales at a relatively low cost, and many businesses have even opted to go fully electronic and close their brick and mortar stores because of the huge cost advantages of selling online. After all, an online store doesn't require a lease, or utilities, or many of the other overhead costs associated with selling in the physical world. That isn't to say you should close down your B&M sales operations, but you should analyze whether or not online sales are a good fit for your business. You may be able to significantly increase your sales.

E-commerce sites require a shopping cart system to be installed on the site. A shopping cart system is essentially a piece of software you install on your site that allows you to add your products to your online store, and allows users to browse those products, add them to their "virtual cart" and then check out and pay. You'll also need to be able to process credit card transactions. This might be something your business is already set up for, and the merchant account provider you use likely has an online solution you can use. Otherwise, there are plenty of online payment options you can use such as PayPal and 2Checkout.

Shipping is something you'll need to deal with if you decide to sell online. No customer is going to want to make their purchase online and then have to go into the store to pick it up (although some larger big-box stores offer this as an option, it needs to be *an* option, and not the only option). So if you don't have a shipping department (or time to do the shipping yourself) then you'll need to consider that. While the customer will pay for shipping as part of their purchase, it can be somewhat time-consuming to package up and ship items without the proper resources.

The beauty of e-commerce sites is that they give the visitor the option to buy right then and there, when their interest is at its highest. If a potential customer comes to your website to research one of your products, goes through your material and decides they want what you're selling, why make them wait? What if it's the weekend and you're not open until Monday? What happens if their desire wanes between now and then? With an e-commerce site, you can give them the option of making their purchase right away. That is a beautiful thing for any business. Part of your job in sales is to build up your customers' desire for your product as much as possible. If your site does that, then being able to get the sale right then and there can be a huge benefit.

Landing Pages/Sales Pages

Landing pages are pages specifically designed for visitors to "land" on from a certain offer. That offer could be an ad on the net that they click on, or a call to action in one of your print materials that gets them to type in a URL. The key with a landing page is that it is very, very specific. It isn't a general page with a lot of information on different things. It's a single page devoted to a single offer, and ideally with a clear action you want the reader to take. For instance, if you're having a special sale on one of your products, you could give it its own landing page specifically for that offer. You can then run a marketing campaign on that offer and direct users to that landing page instead of your main site.

That being said, landing pages aren't generally stand alone sites on their own. They can be, but they work much better as supplements to your main page. The reason for this is that because landing pages are so specific, unless your business sells only one single product or service, a landing page just won't be good enough to serve your entire business. They are so incredibly effective though for promoting individual offers that it's almost frightening. The reason they're so effective is that you're focusing the reader. You're containing them to exactly the offer you want them to see without distracting them in any way.

Search Engine Optimization

S earch engine optimization is one of the most important things that any business can do for their web efforts. The simple reason is, as noted before, local search is quickly moving away from the yellow pages and onto the net in the form of web searches on Google, Bing, Yahoo! and more. If your business isn't showing up prominently in those local searches, then you're missing out big time. That's what search engine optimization (SEO) is all about; getting your site to come up as highly as possible in searches whether they be local or general. Without SEO, you might get lucky and end up with a good position in the search engine results pages (SERPs), but the odds are, you'll end up buried deep down on the third, fourth, fifth or twentieth page. That means you might as well not be there at all. But with carefully done SEO, you'll have a much, much better chance of showing up on the first page, and if you're really good (and a bit lucky on top of that), you might even get that coveted first overall spot!

Search engine optimization revolves around making your site as friendly as possible to search engines such as Google and Microsoft's new Bing search engine. These search engines rank and display the sites you see on any given search results page using incredibly complicated algorithms, proprietary to each search engine, designed to ensure that the best and most valid results possible show up first. These algorithms are so complicated in fact, and so secret, that no one outside of the tech people at the respective companies actually knows exactly how they work. What we do know though, is *parts* of the algorithms. Little bits and pieces of what those algorithms want to see in order to rank sites as highly as possible. These areas are what SEO focuses on. Areas that website owners can specifically target in order to give their site the best shot possible at coming up on top.

These areas are many and the list of different things you can do to optimize your site for search are long and ever changing (one reason it's very important to constantly maintain your SEO efforts to make sure they're up to date). They boil down at the most basic level to two different types of SEO. There is on-page SEO, and off-page SEO. Simply enough, on-page SEO is SEO work done on your actual site, targeting elements within the site like the code, the text, optimized images, and the like. This is the most basic and probably one of the most needlessly ignored areas of SEO. Essentially there is no excuse for any website, especially any business website, to not have good on-page SEO, but almost none do (meaning if yours does, you've got an edge!)

Off-page SEO is work done on *other* sites. Wait, what? Why the heck would doing work on someone else's site help *your* search rankings? Well, the reason is that one of the ways search engines rank your site is by taking into account what others are saying about you, so to speak. Essentially, the way it works is that when another site puts up a link to your site, the search engines take that to mean that there must be something good on your site to deserve that link, and it's sort of like a point in your favor. So the more links you have on other websites across the net, the better you'll look in the eyes of search engines. Enter off-page SEO, which essentially comes down to building those links on other sites around the web. Sounds easy enough right? Build a million links and you'll dominate the search engines! Right? Right?

Unfortunately, it doesn't quite work that way. You see people have tried that, specifically, spammers and garbage websites tried that, building thousands of links on things called 'link farms'. The thing is, Google isn't stupid. In fact they're very smart. That's why they essentially own the world now. So what Google (and most major search engines) do, is to consider the *quality* of a link when factoring it into a site's search ranking. What that means is that a link from CNN or from The New York Times of from the United States Government is worth a *lot* more than a link from Manny's Barbeque Sauce Blog or IsntMyCatCute.com. This is the tricky part. Everybody and their brother wants to get links from these high quality sites, or 'authority sites' as they're often called. And so these sites don't just give out links. Well, actually they do, but not the kind you want for SEO.

Ugh, now there are different *types* of links? You betcha! The internet runs on links, they're everywhere, and for the millions of sites out there, there are millions more links floating around on them. And so the guys who run the complicated innards of the internet invented what are known as do-follow and no-follow links. Simply enough, a do-follow link counts for search engine rankings, and a no-follow link doesn't. So when most of the really good sites give out links, they're no-follow, and they absolutely don't matter for a thing as far as search ranking goes. They're still good because any link that allows a person to find your site is a good thing, but as far as SEO goes, they're not worth the font they're written in.

So to be successful in off-page SEO, you need to find strong, high quality links, from authority sites that the search engines give a lot of weight to, that are also do-follow. It's doable, but definitely not easy. Then add to that all the on-page SEO factors like page titles, header tags, keywords, etc., and you've got quite a full plate. The good news though is that if you get the mix right, you can get your sites ranking in good spots on search results pages. In fact you can even choose the specific terms you optimize your site for to ensure that you're showing up properly in the *right* searches to maximize your sites effectiveness.

This is where the local vs. global thing comes into play. When targeting the key phrases you want to optimize your site for (key phrases basically just means 'what people type into Google') you need to decide whether or not you want to target large, broad key phrases, or more local, more specific key phrases. For instance, do you optimize your site for the search term 'car repair', or for the search term 'Sacramento Auto Body Work'? At first this might seem like an obvious choice; go big or go home, right? The broader search term 'car repair' will deliver way more traffic, so go for that one! Well the problem with that is that while, yes, the term 'car repair' almost certainly gets a great deal more searches than the other term, it's also extremely competitive. With SEO, the more generic a search phrase is, the more competition there will be, and for really broad search terms, the sites sitting at the tops of those rankings are going to be extremely, extremely hard to knock off.

For instance, let's say you own a small independent movie theatre in Toronto and you want to do some SEO for your website.

You decide to target the term 'movie theatre'. After all, it'll get a ton of searches! Unfortunately, the websites sitting at the top of the search results for 'movie theatre' belong to Cineplex, Empire Theatres, MovieTickets.com, AMC, Movie Fone, and the like. See the problem? I don't care how hard you try, you are *not* going to knock off AMC and Cineplex from the top of the rankings with the site for your small local theatre. Well, it's possible I suppose, but absolutely not worth the ridiculous amount of effort and money it would take.

So instead of targeting such a ridiculously competitive phrase, you target a more specific, more local phrase. You absolutely won't get as much traffic, but the traffic the search term does get will be far more *targeted*. Ah, targeting, the marketers best friend! Remember, you're a small independent theatre in Toronto. Why do you want someone in Georgia to come to your website? Or someone in France? That's exactly what will happen if you somehow succeed in making the first page for the term 'movie theatre'. So forget that one and instead let's target 'Toronto Independent Theatre'. Now there's a search phrase you can dig into! It's far less competitive, meaning it's very realistic to think you can get into the top of the rankings. Not only that, but now you know that the people finding your site through Google are people looking specifically for what *you* provide.

Now you're marketing to people looking for a small independent theatre in Toronto. Not people looking for a large super-

theater in Florida. Remember what we said way back about marketing only to people who want to see your marketing messages and not wasting your time on those that don't? This is a perfect example and that's exactly why targeting more specific key phrases (what are often known as 'long tail key phrases') is of so much value. Firstly because it qualifies your leads much better, and secondly because it ensures that the people who end up finding your site are the people who *want* to find what your site has to offer. Someone who doesn't want what you're hawking will leave your site before it even finishes loading, so why waste time and money marketing to them? Focusing on long tail key phrases and local search strings lets you laser focus your marketing, which ultimately makes it more effective.

Google Positioning:

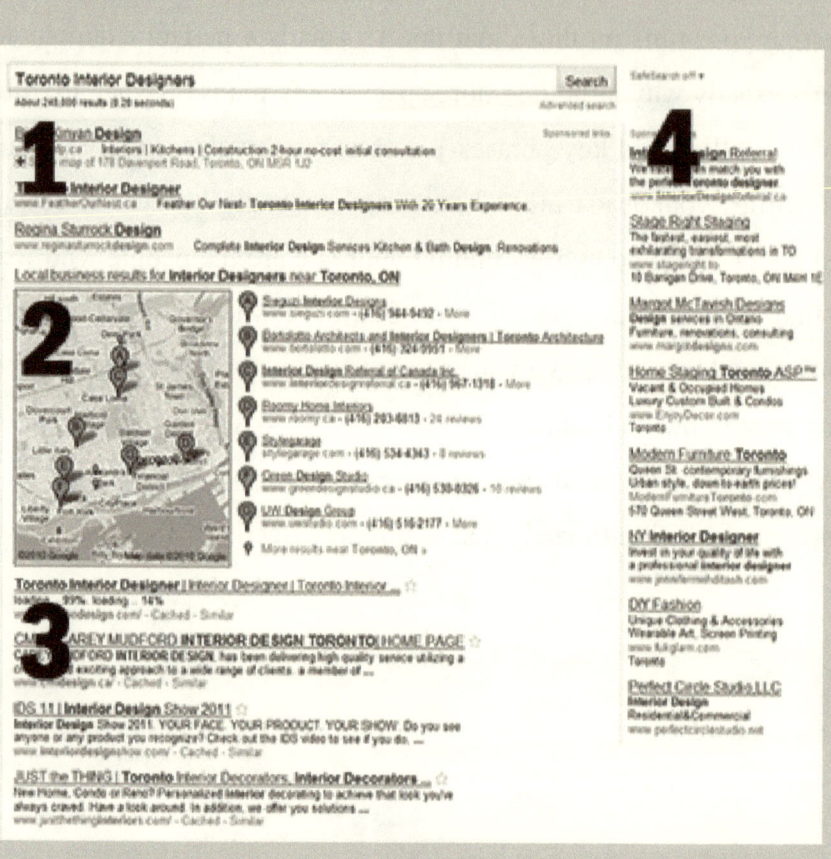

1) Paid search results.

2) Google Places local business listings. This is the bread and butter when it comes to Google and local business. If you can get your business to show up prominently here you'll be set.

3) Google organic search results. This is the next most important place to be for most local businesses. The top three positions in the organic results get the vast majority of clicks.

4) Paid search results.

Web Metrics

Web metrics are the secret of what makes marketing on the internet so effective both from a campaign success perspective and from a cost perspective. When you market on the web, the amount of data you can get back out of your campaigns is absolutely mind boggling, and using that data, you can literally figure out just about anything you could possibly want to about how your campaigns are working (or aren't working). By studying these metrics, you can adjust your campaign and fine tune it to work as well as possible and also to be as cheap as possible. Whether it be your copy, your targeting, your delivery medium, your website or landing page, or any other aspect of your online marketing efforts, your metrics will show you (with a little skillful interpretation), *exactly* what you want (and need) to know to succeed. Can your offline marketing do that? I don't think so.

Your metrics are provided in a few different ways depending on what aspects of your campaign you're looking it. Your website will have one set of data you can look at, your online ad campaigns will provide another set, etc. Often times these different areas can be integrated so that your numbers for each can be compared and contrasted with each other, giving you a fuller picture of your overall marketing efforts. You don't have to spend a lot of money to get these different sets of analytics, in fact, some of the best packages are completely free to use, you just need to know how to set them up and get them started. The following are some of the different areas you can use metrics to analyze, and the specific types of data that they'll give you.

Website Analytics

Website analytics will tell you about how your website is performing in a multitude of different ways. They can give you insight on everything from how your site should be organized, to which areas of the site visitors spend the most time on, to how they move through it, to overall traffic numbers and much more. Google Analytics is a free web analytics package provided by Google which can be installed on your website for free and setup to provide you with all this information. There are also paid options for analytics packages that work equally well, if not slightly better, but the quality of data Google Analytics provides at no cost makes it a favorite for most applications. Here are just *some* of the types of data you can get from these packages;

Visits: This describes the number of gross visits that your site receives from web users.

Unique Visitors: Visits will double count the same person if they come to your website more than once in the same day with a gap in between. The unique visitors stat eliminates this double counting and tells you exactly how many unique individuals came to your site in a given period. This is highly valuable since it's essential you know how much traffic is coming through your site each day.

Pageviews: Pageviews tells you the number of individual pages on your site a visitor sees. If a person comes to your site and clicks through 10 pages, they'll count as one unique visitor, and 10 pageviews.

New Visits: The new visits metric tells you the percentage of people coming to your site who have never been there before. This is incredibly important for a couple of reasons. One, you obviously want to know how many new potential clients are finding your site, but you also want to know if people *aren't* returning. If your site has a very high percentage of new visitors compared to returning visitors, then you'll need to examine *why* people aren't coming back.

Average Time on Site: This well tell you how long the average visitor spends on your site. Obviously if this is only a matter of seconds, that tells you a lot!

Geographical Location: Your analytics package can tell you where your visitors and prospects are coming from on scales both large and small. You can narrow down location by country, state, and city. This is obviously very valuable information, especially for businesses that sell across State or Provincial lines.

Traffic Sources: This metric tells you exactly where your visitors are coming from. If your visitors are coming from a link on another website, an email campaign, an ad campaign, or a number of other sources, it'll tell you where they came from and how they got to your site. This is very important since it gives you the ability to narrow down and target your best traffic sources so you can eliminate the ones that don't work and put extra focus on the ones that do.

Keywords: This tells you which keywords and key phrases visitors used when finding your sites through search engines. This combined with data from some other sources is incredibly valuable to your online ad campaigns as well as your search engine optimization efforts, since you can determine what key phrases you're ranking well for and which ones you aren't ranking well for.

Navigation Analysis: This lets you see which pages on your site visitors are coming from when jumping to other pages, and where they're most likely to go next.

Entrance and Exit Pages: This metric shows you which pages visitors are landing on when entering your site, and more importantly, which pages on your site they're leaving from. If they're leaving at a point you don't want them to, something needs to change!

Goals Tracking: This is one of the most powerful areas in the Google Analytics package. This metric allows you to set up your site in order to track the movements of your prospects through your sales funnel. This provides incredibly valuable insight into where along your sales funnel prospects are dropping out.

Custom Reporting: Custom reporting allows you to set up your own custom reports that will focus on only the areas you're most interested in analyzing, leaving out those you aren't interested in. This is valuable since the sheer amount of data provided is large, and it's nice to not have to sift through all of it when you don't need to.

Ad Campaign Analytics

Another area where you can get very detailed analytics to help you with your marketing is online ad campaigns. Online advertising, including pay-per click, cost per mille (per thousand impressions), and more will all provide you with significant stats regarding how your online efforts are performing. Here are some of the metrics you can analyze when examining your online ad campaigns;

Impressions: Impressions tells you the number of times you're ad has been served. Every time a web user sees your ad it is counted as an impression. This isn't the same as a unique impression, because raw impressions counts page reloads, multiple pages and return visitors, meaning your raw impressions is much higher than unique. Impressions are essentially the same as page views, but for an ad rather than a web page. If you're paying for your ads on a CPM basis (cost per 1000 impressions), then this is an extremely important number for you since it determines what your cost to run the ad is.

Clicks: This number tells you how many times the visitors who saw your ad actually clicked on it and went through to your website or offer. This is a very important stat for a couple of reasons. First of all, if you're running your ads on pay per click system, then you'll be paying each time someone clicks your ad, so those clicks are your cost driver. Secondly, your ad is only doing its job if people *are* clicking on it, so determining your number of clicks is an important step in determining your ads success.

Click Through Rate: You click through rate (CTR) is the percentage of impressions that turn into clicks. You simply divide your clicks by your impressions to get your CTR. A low CTR tells you that your ad isn't performing well for what could be a number of reasons. It could be that you ad copy simply isn't compelling enough, or it could be that you have good copy but your ad's targeting needs to be improved. CTR is a very important metric and often times, you're better off working on your CTR rather than trying to drive more traffic to your ad or site.

Cost Per Click: Your cost per click (CPC) is the price you pay each time someone clicks on one of your ads. This will normally be paid to the ad network that is serving your ads, or if you're doing your advertising independently, directly to the sites hosting your ads. Cost per click is one of the most important metrics to analyze when examining the cost effectiveness of your campaigns because often times, by improving your ad and improving your targeting, you can drive your CPC down to a lower rate than it is currently at. Nailing your CPC down to the lowest point possible is a key to maximizing profit.

Conversions: Conversions indicate how many times your ad clicks result in the visitor taking the desired action you've set out. That could mean they click through to your site and sign up for your mailing list, or that they click through and purchase a specific product. This is an important indicator of how well your ad, your copy and your offer are working together. For instance, if you have a large number of visitors clicking on your ads and going through to your offer, but then very few actually taking action on that offer, that tells you there is a problem in one of a few possible areas. It could be that your ad's copy and your offer's copy don't synch up well enough which is causing confusion among your visitors. Or it could just be that your offer simply needs to be better. Either way, being able to accurately track conversions is extremely helpful in ensuring your campaigns are as profitable as possible.

Email Analytics

Email campaigns are one of the best ways a business can stay connected with their existing customers as well as reach out to potential new customers. By maintaining and building a mailing list, you can keep in constant contact with your subscribers, building trust and ensuring they think of you first when they need products or services you provide. Like everything else though, your email campaigns can't reach their full potential without tracking their performance. Here are some of the metrics you can examine using the analytics packages that come with most auto-responder packages;

New Subscribers: This metric will give you insight into how many new subscribers have signed up to receive your newsletters or emails. You can view new subscribers on a daily, weekly or yearly basis, giving you a great deal of insight into when your list building efforts are performing at their best.

Subscribe Method: There are a few ways that users can sign up to your mailing list and this metric will show you exactly where you're getting your largest number of sign-ups from. Users can sign up for your list through an online form on a website, which is the most common way of gaining new subscribers, or they can email your auto-responder address to automatically include themselves. Finally, you can import subscribers manually from existing mailing lists you may already have.

Ad Tracking: This feature lets you determine not just *how* your subscribers sign up for your list, but *where* they sign up from. For instance, you might have two opt in forms, one on your main website and one on a landing page for one of your ad campaigns. You might also put up ads in online classifieds with a subscription link. Using ad tracking, you can keep track of which of these avenues each of your subscribers come through, allowing you to pinpoint which methods are seeing the most success.

Geographical Location: Geographical location tracking tells you where your subscribers are located. You can narrow down your geographical tracking on a number of levels. For instance the AWeber auto-responder package allows you to break down geographical location by country, state/province, cities, area codes (the 30 most popular) and Designated Market Area codes (the 30 most popular).

Message Tracking: Message tracking allows you to measure the performance of your individual messages. By examining metrics such as the open rate of the messages, and the number of clicks on the links inside each message, you can determine which of your emails are having the most success. For instance, a message with a very low open rate is often suffering from a lack luster title. You can then identify which titles have given you the highest open rates in the past, and re-craft the under-performing message's title in the same fashion.

The Google Analytics Interface

Google Analytics provides a very straight forward way to analyze your websites traffic and the way that traffic interacts with your site and your business. Charts, graphs, maps and more all make it easy to visually analyze trends in recent activity, and the data provides goes into incredible depth.

Enterprise analytics like those provides by Google are of incredible value to business who wish to improve their systems and in the end bring in more sale. Remember, you can't manage what you can't measure, and unless you're actively tracking and collecting data about your business, its systems and its successes, then you can never be sure whether or not you're meeting your full potential.

Section Three

Advertising and Generating New Business

Advertising Your Business Online

So now you've got your website up and running, it's got a great design, it's optimized for search engines, and it has all the information a prospective customer could ever want. So now what? Well you have a couple of option. The first is to just allow it to sit there and do nothing else. If your website has been well optimized for local search, then you should see some traffic start to come in from Google, Bing, etc. This is what you call organic search traffic. Its traffic that found your site through search without any outside influence, and this is a great kind of traffic, but it isn't the only kind. You don't just have to let your website operate on a proverbial island removed from any extra assistance on your part. Why not advertise your business online and drive some traffic to that shiny new website? Traffic that, if obtained correctly, should result in extra revenues!

Welcome to the wonderful world of online advertising! Advertising online serves the exact same purpose that advertising on television, radio, billboards and bus stations serves. The goal is to generate business. Ideally, people will see your ad, follow up on it in one way or another, sooner or later, and in the end, put money in your pocket. But as we've discussed in previous chapters, online advertising comes with the added benefit of being incredibly measurable. So really, if you're advertising in the offline world, you owe it to your business to examine your options in the online world, because you could stand to profit handsomely from reaching out and touching those online prospects with an ad or two.

If you're still living in the age where you associate online advertising with 'SPAM', then it's time to realize that advertising online is a completely legitimate medium and one that some of the biggest companies in the world make use of. While those companies spend millions and millions of dollars to advertise on some of the most popular websites on the internet, you can just as easily make very good use of online advertising with the kinds of budgets that most small businesses have available. In fact, because of the exceptional targeting potential of online advertising, along with the detailed metrics that it provides, advertising online is actually often significantly cheaper than advertising through other popular mediums.

So if well designed and well delivered online advertising

campaign can generate as much or more business than offline campaigns, at a significantly lower cost, why isn't *your* business making use of this great medium? Well, the fact of the matter is that most small businesses and small business owners just don't quite understand the power it has, or exactly how to utilize it. In the following sections we'll look at the ins and outs of online advertising. By the end of it, you'll almost certainly have some ideas about how you can use it to further your own company's success.

Targeting on the Web

Targeting is the act of focusing your ads on certain groups and demographics in order to maximize your chances for success. Targeting is one of the single most important aspects of marketing and advertising because without it, a business will be blasting out its marketing messages at random. Sure, some of the right people will be exposed to them, but every time those messages go out to the wrong eyes or wrong ears, it's money down the drain. Why bother identifying demographics to describe your ideal customers if you don't then look for ways to incorporate them into your campaigns as much as possible? Fortunately, the web shines when it comes to targeting, and by learning to use the web's targeting power effectively, you can move your business into a world where it spends *less* money on marketing but brings in *more* sales.

Depending on the type of advertising you're using, the web allows you to target your efforts with laser like precision. For instance, advertisers who choose to use Facebook ads as a method of getting their message out will find themselves hit with a ridiculous amount of targeting options. At the time of writing this, those options include; location (down to city level), age range, exact birthday, gender, educational level, workplaces, relationship status, sexual orientation, languages, connections and keywords. As you can see, this kind of targeting is an incredibly powerful tool. In the offline world, if your ideal prospect is a male aged 25 to 35, who is married and has a college education, you could put your ads out there in the places where those types of people would be most likely to see them, but you could never really be 100% certain. On the web, you can target your ad in such a way that you have near 100% certainty that the only people seeing it, and therefore the only people you're spending advertising dollars to reach, are *exactly* who you're trying to get through to.

Not all advertising platforms offer this kind of targeting bundled in one place, but almost across the board, web advertising beats out offline advertising for targeting capability. Whether it be targeting your messages by geographical location, age range, interests, or whatever else you can think of, on the web, there *will* be some way of reaching your target demographics very specifically and with a great deal of measurability. Throughout the following chapters we'll make note of the targeting capabilities of each type of advertising medium that we discuss so that you'll have a better overall idea of which types of advertising offer the most accurate targeting.

Regardless of what type of online advertising your company goes with, it's essential that you take whatever targeting is available to you and use it to its full extent. There is simply no excuse not to. If your company is about to dive into online marketing and advertising, and you don't yet have a clear picture of your target demographics or ideal customer, you'll want to spend some time nailing those down first in order to be able to take full advantage of the power of targeted advertising on the internet.

Local Advertising

L ocal customers are the lifeblood of the vast most small and medium businesses. For most small businesses, there is no other type of customer and reaching out to them is the key to success. Luckily, online advertising is an incredibly effective way to reach out to your local customer base, both existing clients and potential clients. Because of the amazing degree with which online campaigns can be narrowed down, you can target you're ad campaigns to very specific geographical locations, ensuring that you aren't wasting any time or effort on users who are outside of your range. It's just one more using the web is a great way of ensuring that your marketing and advertising efforts are being target specifically to only the most qualified prospects.

Google Business Center

One of the simplest and most effective ways of advertising to your local client base is also completely free (and once again, provided by your friends at Google!) The Google Business Center is like the Yellow Pages on crack. It's a directory, much like the Yellow Pages are, but it combines the power of a directory with the amazing reach of Google search. Utilizing the Google business center is incredibly important for a couple of reasons. First of all, when you enter your business with the Local Business Center, your business will show up on Google maps searches.

Google Maps is the most popular online map and direction site on the net, and a great deal of people use it every day to find directions from point A to point B. But people also use it to look up what businesses are in and around their local areas. For instance, if you type in "restaurants in Orlando, Florida", Google Maps will provide you with a graphical map with a whole bunch of little pins each representing a local restaurant. Zoom in further, or put in a more specific search term like "restaurants near Lake Eola Park", you'll get the same results but narrowed down even further. This means when someone does this for your area, if your business isn't listed, you'll be handing over prospective customers to your competitors that *are* listed!

But the real power of Google Business Center comes from the way it interacts with Google's search engine. That same map that people see when they search through Google Maps also comes up in Google's search results when people do a search straight through the search engine. The same map (but smaller) along with a list of the businesses shown (and short descriptions) shows up, and best of all, it shows up *at the top*! This means that if you can get your business into a prominent position in these free local business listings, that when people in your area search for a local company providing what your company provides, you'll show up right at the top of the search results, even above the normal organic results.

This is *extremely* powerful because this is where the majority of internet searchers are going to look to when searching for local businesses. Often times, they may not even bother looking further down the page, they'll simply select one of the top businesses in the local search results and click through to that company's website. So you can easily understand why it's so important for your business to show up in those local search listings. In fact, getting yourself positioned well in those local business listings might actually be the *most important* thing your business does to advertise itself (assuming that is that your potential customers are primarily local).

Paid Local Advertising

There are also other options for local advertising that businesses can use such as Google AdWords or Facebook ads in order to reach out to potential customers. With both of these services, and a host of other options like them, the key to their successful use is that they offer an extremely high degree of targeting. You can target not only by location down to the city level, but also through other means such as demographics like age, marital status, or many others, and by focusing on specific keywords. These contextual advertising services provide businesses with a fantastic, and very inexpensive, method of reach potential customers. Possibly the most powerful of which is pay per click advertising including (and especially) Google AdWords, which we'll cover in the next chapter, so read on.

Pay per Click Advertising

Pay per click advertising is one of the most widely used forms of advertising that exists on the web. Users of pay per click (PPC) include Fortune 500 corporations and one man home businesses alike. The reason that so many businesses both small and large use PPC is very simple; it works. Regardless of the scale that it's being done on, pay per click advertising, when done right, is a very effective and very profitable way of reaching out to potential customers. PPC has a very wide reach, is effective in its simplicity, and offers very good analytics. It isn't the best option for all businesses, but most can work it into their advertising mix. However, for many businesses, effective PPC campaigns can be the difference between profit and loss, or between mediocre results and huge results.

If you've ever used Google then you've seen pay per click advertising. When you do a Google you'll see the organic search results, which are the websites that come up (normally 10) on each results page. But for most common terms you'll also see a set of results either directly above the common terms, or more commonly off to the right hand side. These results are advertisements from the Google AdWords network, which is just one (and the biggest) of the many pay per click ad networks that exist. Those ads have been placed there by businesses or individuals, and every time someone clicks one of those ads and goes through to the website that the ad links to, the business that placed the ad pays a fee to Google.

The way PPC works is that businesses bid on specific keywords and key phrases that they want their ads to be displayed for. For instance, if a business sells racecar beds, then they might bid on the term "racecar beds", so that every time someone goes to Google to search for that term, their ad will show up right alongside the organic search results and ideally, the user will click through their ad and go on to their website. If that business was located in Indianapolis, they might bid on the term "Indianapolis racecar beds" so that their ad would show up specifically for searches for racecar beds located in Indianapolis. The number of different keywords and key phrases a business can bid on is limited only by their imaginations, and sometimes, the most successful keywords are far from the most obvious ones.

The reason for this is that the price a business pays for each click is based off a bidding system, so how much or little a business pays is controlled largely by how many other businesses also want to use those same keywords. So if only one business or individual is bidding on the phrase "Indianapolis racecar beds", then the cost per click (CPC), which is the price paid for each click, will be relatively low (sometimes even as low as just a few cents!) However, if there are swarms of competition all trying to bid on that phrase, then the cost will rise. If you want your ad to show up on the first page of results (where it is most likely to be clicked), then you'll need to outbid that competition. Some highly competitive terms (normally in medical and legal fields) have incredibly high CPC's, sometimes $20 or more!

This is where PPC strategy starts to come in! As you can see, if you just bid on all the popular terms, the ones that are getting the most searches, and the most competition, you'll probably find yourself needing to bid high amounts for your clicks, and that can get expensive fast. So you need to do two things; first, you need to analyze the more popular, more expensive keywords to figure out if they're worth your trouble at all. Sometimes they aren't, but sometimes they are. A high CPC doesn't necessarily mean a keyword won't be highly profitable for you. The second thing is to look for lower cost keywords, and the way to do this is to get specific, and the more specific the better (within reason of course).

What that means is to look for something called 'long-tail keywords'. Long tail keywords are simply longer, more specific keywords, usually containing at least three words, and often even more. So for instance whereas 'racecar beds' is a short-tail keyword, "Indianapolis racecar beds" is a long tail keyword. You could go even longer and go for "red Indianapolis racecar beds". The difference between long-tail keywords and short-tail keywords is that long-tail keywords are generally cheaper, more targeted, and also get less search volume. So while you'll normally pay less per click for long tail keywords, those keywords will also get less searches, and therefore less clicks overall. However, those cheaper clicks you *do* get, will be more targeted than clicks on a more general keyword.

So overall, long-tail keywords are good. In fact, they're great. Because if you can find some good ones, you'll be paying rock bottom prices for very targeted traffic, and that is the ultimate goal when it comes to PPC advertising. By narrowing down the traffic you're paying for through PPC by using longer tail keywords, you're helping to qualify those leads to ensure that you aren't paying for clicks that aren't any good to you. For instance, if that company that sells racecar beds only sells them in blue, then they're wasting their money paying for clicks from people looking to buy red racecar beds. If they bid on the term "racecar beds", they'll almost certainly end up with a lot of traffic from people looking to buy red ones. By instead bidding on "blue racecar beds", they can be sure each person clicking through to their website is looking for exactly what it is they have to sell, and that they aren't wasting money paying for clicks that have no chance of converting.

So as you can see, by focusing on long-tail keywords, that racecar bed business eliminates the possibility of spending big money on high CPC visitors who aren't even looking for what they're selling. They've dodged one of the biggest dangers of PPC advertising! Now, instead of going broke paying for traffic they can't convert, they're instead spending very little on traffic that can. Remember, there is effectively very little difference between 100 visitors of which only 10% are qualified, and 10 visitors of which 100% are qualified. You've got the same number of qualified prospects either way. The big difference is that those 100 general visitors, driven to your site by a short-tail keyword like "racecar bed" might cost a dollar each, whereas the 10 from "blue racecar bed" might only cost 20 cents each. So one method gets you 10 qualified leads for $100, and one gets you 10 qualified leads for $20! You can imagine the cost difference this makes on a large scale campaign.

As discussed in the metrics section, PPC normally gives you very good data on how your campaigns are performing. It's a good thing too because with PPC, the key is testing, analyzing and optimizing your campaigns. You'll never get the best price results right off the bat when you start a campaign. That's because some keywords won't perform as well as you thought, and some will. Some will need to have their bids tweaked up to get the traffic you want, and some will present room to lower your bid, which will save you money. For this reason it's incredibly important that companies looking to get into PPC have it managed by someone on staff or someone external to the company that understand PPC in great depth. If PPC is done wrong, it can bleed money fast and end up being costly rather than profitable. But done right, PPC is a great source of traffic for your website and leads for your business, and can result in great increases to sales and profits.

Article Marketing

Article marketing is the process of writing short articles to publish on the web as a way to promote your business. Article marketing does a couple of things for you that make it a valuable promotional tool for many businesses. First of all, article marketing builds up the back links to your website. From a purely SEO point of view, this is important because it helps search engines identify your site as "trusted" by the net (re-read the search engine optimization chapter if you need a refresher). This will help boost your sites within the systems of Google and other similar search engines.

Secondly, article marketing sends traffic directly to your site. When you write your promotional articles you include links back to your website or offer, and if you do your job right, readers will click those links and navigate through to where you want them to go. Finally, article marketing helps establish you as an authority in your industry.

Much like writing articles for trade publications, if you publish your online articles in the right places, the reputation they bring you could be highly valuable.

There are a few places you can publish your articles in order to bring in traffic and increase your authority on a subject. The main three are on your own site, on article directories, and on authority sites relating to your niche. These are the big three, and while there is some debate on which the best are and which will provide the most benefits to your business, any of the three will generally be beneficial, and each one has different benefits and different drawbacks.

On Your Own Site:

Publishing on your own site (or on your company's blog) has the major benefit of ensuring that *all* the traffic that comes to your articles is also traffic for your own sites. When you submit to an article directory, you might get more traffic to your article, but that article is published on someone else's website. You're essentially providing valuable content for someone else's website rather than your own. By publishing on your own site, that content is yours, and when it gets indexed in the search engines, those results will point right back to your site. The downside is that you won't get as much traffic from the articles as you would by publishing them on one of the other options.

Article Directories:

Publishing in the major article directories has a lot of benefits. While it's true that by publishing in directories you're providing content for someone else's website, that doesn't really matter, as long as you can make that content work for your own site's benefit. When you publish on directories, you can do that in two ways. Firstly, the directories are considered high authority sites by Google, and so the links you gain from your articles published on the directory provide you with high authority back links which are valuable for SEO. Secondly, the links you place in your articles, when clicked, will take the readers back to your company's website.

It may seem counter intuitive to publish content on someone else's site in order to hopefully bring them back to your own, but it isn't. The reason being is that the article directories get *a lot* of traffic, and the odds are your article published on a top directory will get more readers than it would published on your own site. So if you can write a good article that converts (draws readers into clicking your link) at a reasonable rate, then you'll actually end up with more traffic than you would if you'd published on your own site. For instance, at the time of writing this, this author has had 298 short articles (between 250 and 500 words) published on one of the top article directories. Those articles have received 98,707 views, and out of those, readers have clicked through to my sites 20,833 times.

Authority Sites in Your Niche:

Writing for authority sites in your niche is essentially the exact same principal as writing articles for trade publications or popular magazines relating to your business. The only real difference is that one is in print and one is digital. That, and the fact that it is often *much* easier to get published online than it is to get published in the print world. Websites are driven by content, and sites are constantly hungry for new material. This is a significant opportunity for you and your business to turn that need for content into authority and traffic for your own business and website.

By writing articles for these authority sites in your niche you benefit yourself in much the same way that you do when publishing in article directories. Most of these authority sites are considered in high regard by Google's fancy algorithms, and so the links you'll gain are highly valuable. Secondly, those links will point readers back to your own website (assuming you've written your article in such a way as to draw them to click those links – a skill in itself). The drawback to posting on these sites is that for reasons we won't bother getting into (technical mumbo jumbo), the links from these sites sometimes don't count for SEO purposes. However, the benefit is that because these sites are authority sites within the specific industry or niche you sell in, the readers you're getting are probably more targeted than the reader you'd get through an article directory.

Regardless of where you publish, the key to having success when using article marketing is to write articles that provide actual useful information to your readers, but also leave them hungry for more. Without doing that, you'll never get them to click on your links and navigate through to your own site. If you're writing for directories, you'll want to write shorter articles. If you're writing for an authority site in your industry, how long your articles are will depend really on what they need. They could ask you for a feature length article, in which case you can pour out a short essay if you want, or they could ask you for a small sidebar piece. Remember though, readers on the net generally don't read as long as they would offline, so making your articles too long can actually be just as bad as making them too short! Anyway you look at it though, article marketing is a fairly effective way to market, and best of all, it doesn't cost you a penny!

Articles Succeeding In Google

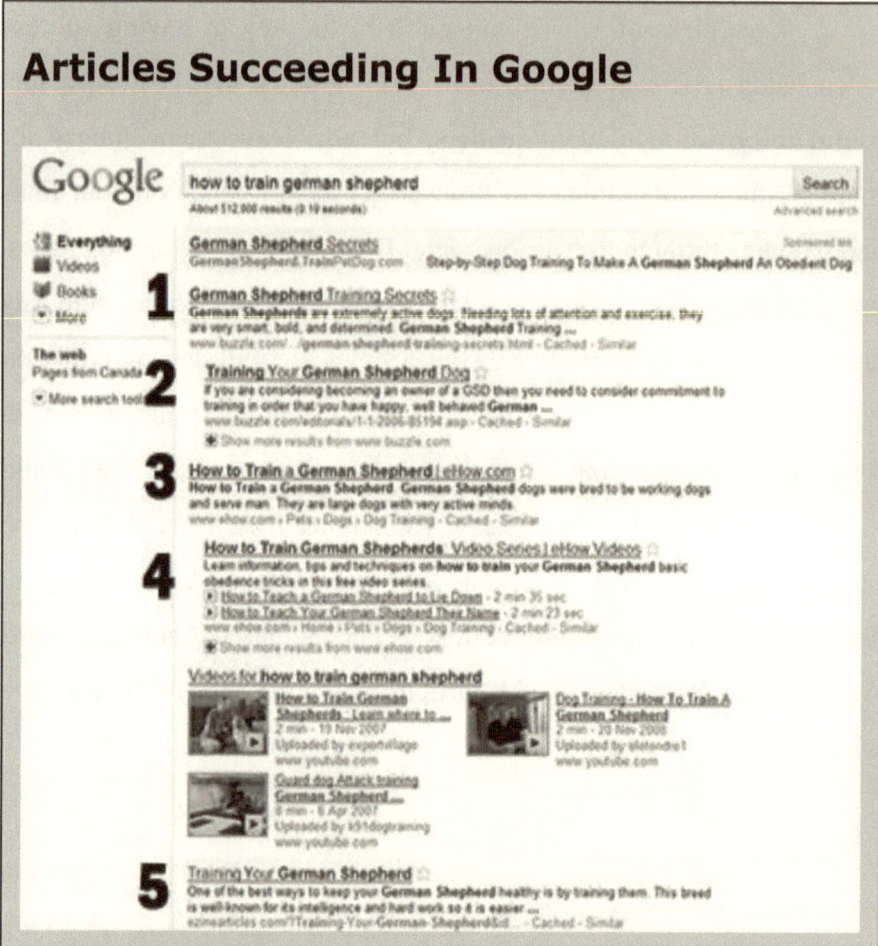

Here is an example of a high traffic search term showing 5 article directory articles as the top 5 organic search terms. (note that the other 3 are videos, another form of digital marketing medium!)

Dog training is a niche made up of near fanatical customers (pet lovers). So here you have a search term where someone is clearly looking for dog training, and 5 articles from article directories are the sites pulling in the vast majority of those

Online Direct Mail

irect mail is used in the offline world because it's a proven winner. The costs associated with doing a large scale mailing are relatively low, and if your copy and offer are compelling enough, you can normally assure yourself a success rate high enough to make your campaigns profitable. If you're really good at it, the effectiveness becomes almost scary, and some of the gurus of direct mail get staggering response rates. But direct mail doesn't have to be exclusive to the realm of offline marketing. You can run very effective direct mail campaigns online too, just with emails instead of postcards and letters. The response rates can be just as high, the costs associated with sending out large numbers of mailings are just as low, and just like with most aspects of online marketing, you have more options when it comes to targeting.

You'll need to find a list of people to email to that suits the needs of your campaign. This can be a little tricky because mass emailing people who don't want to be emailed is SPAM and it's not only annoying, it's illegal. So the key is to only mail to people who have clearly indicated that they *want* to receive the messages. You can buy email lists but they're not the most effective way of doing it, and you can never be really certain how many of them are inactive, or if your messages will be flagged as SPAM, and most of the addresses will be junk prospects anyways, so you're better off staying away from buying lists.

Your best bet is instead to approach the owners of websites relating to your industry that have their own well established lists. Often times list owners will be willing to send out a promotional message on behalf of another company for a fee (or a cut of the sales generated from the mailing), and this route is a much better option. First of all, because the list is specific to your industry or niche, you can be more certain that the recipients will be likely to be interested in your offer. Secondly, you can be sure that the recipients won't consider your mailing as SPAM. Well established lists will be made up of subscribers who have opted in to be part of that mailing program, so you can be sure they want to receive emails. This means you won't have people flagging your emails as SPAM, which could get you into a lot of trouble.

Once you've secured a list to do your mailing to, the aspects of a good email mailing are very much the same as those of their offline equivalents. You'll need a good offer, compelling copy and a strong call to action. Try and target your offer as much as possible to cater to the list you're mailing to. The list owner will normally be able to provide you with demographic information about the list so that you can try and tailor your offer as best as possible. And possibly most importantly of all, you'll need an incredibly catchy title for your mailing. People tend to be anxious to open their snail mail, but with email anything that seems promotional will have a hard time getting opened. Unless, that is, your title is compelling enough to make the recipients *need* to open your email.

That's your goal, to make your prospective reader feel like they'll be missing out by *not* opening your email, and then once you've got them to open it, you use standard copywriting techniques to hold their interest, get them *wanting* your offer, and then finally to take action and do whatever it is you want them to do, whether it be just asking for more information or making a purchase. Using email lists in this way provides many of the same benefits that standard snail mail direct mail does, however, be warned, the success rates for online direct mail are significantly lower than they are for most offline mailings. That's ok though because the costs are low enough to make up for that one downside.

Utilizing Video

Video is the new king of the web and the power that video holds is absolutely incredible to behold. Web users eat up video at a ridiculously alarming rate, and some of the most popular sites on the internet today are video sharing sites such as YouTube. Purchased by Google in 2006 for 1.65 billion dollars, YouTube now serves up over *one billion video views each day*! That is an absolutely staggering number of views, and other sites like Google Videos and countless other niche video sites are also serving up millions and millions of views each day. There are a lot of reasons people love video on the web. For one thing, it's normally entertaining and watching video online is becoming as common as watching television or DVDs at home.

Another reason is that video doesn't require reading, and this can be a huge benefit. If you were to transcribe a five minute video and ask a web user to read it, they'd probably get bored and quit half way through, but yet they'll gladly watch the entire five minute video. Video is just a less intensive way to get your message across and so people respond very well to video, and this applies to marketing messages just as much as it does to entertainment. Remember how many times we've talked about engaging your audience when delivering marketing messages? Well video is perfect for that. A big block of text is impersonal and lacks interactivity. Video on the other hand has imagery and dialogue. Even when it is *completely impersonal* a video still engages the viewer on a certain level that text can have a very hard time achieving.

There are a few ways you can utilize video in your marketing and each way is very powerful in its own right. The first way is in your direct response marketing. When you do online direct response marketing, whether it be through email or using landing pages and sales letters, a general rule of thumb is that the higher priced the item you're selling is, the more information you need to present your prospect in order for them to be confident enough to make a purchase. Now if you're selling items for a couple of dollars that might not require much, but as the prices get higher and higher, the amount of text you need becomes larger and larger. I'm sure you've seen those long sales letters online (or in magazine ads or print materials).

They're long because they *need to be*. They need to be because they know that you won't make a purchase unless you're sure of what they're selling, and that takes some convincing.

But what if instead of a 20,000 word sales letter that takes 40 minutes to read, you could present all of that information in an interesting, attention grabbing, interactive way? Say hello to video! You can still use the text, but try making it secondary. Place it starting further down the page and place a video front and center in front of your prospects. Instead of a formula like headline → sub-headline → deck copy → body, try something like headline → sub-headline → video → deck copy → body. This way your prospect has the option to read the long sales copy, or they can watch the video (or a combination of both). What will often happen is the prospect will watch your video, and then scroll down through the sales copy for more information on parts of the video that have peaked their interest.

As good as video is though, one warning, not everyone is video friendly on the internet. In order to really enjoy video, a user needs to have a high speed connection. If they're using a dial up connection, the amount of time it will take for a video to load becomes a huge turn off, and most will just navigate away if there isn't an alternative like text for them to read. Broadband usage is on a steady and steep incline, so for the most part, video is a safe and great way to market, but you should always provide an alternative for those users with slower internet connections. They may want to buy too, and if you only offer video and they can't watch it, you may have just lost a customer!

Video is also a great way to provide information on your products and services to potential customers in an informative setting rather than a sales setting. You can use video to demonstrate product features, different uses for products, to demonstrate a service you provide, to provide technical support, and the list goes on and on. Anything you would demonstrate to a potential customer in person can be (and often should be) available for them to view as a video on the web. Providing this kind of material helps build a rapport between your business and prospective customers without the need to meet them in person. This can provide an incredible number of benefits from further qualifying prospects to help them get into a buying mindset, to reducing the strain on your customer service or technical help.

Finally, video is a great way to produce brand awareness through the production of viral videos. Viral videos are videos, normally of a funny or outrageous nature, that spread throughout the internet like a "virus" (hence the name). Viral videos are incredibly effective *when they work*, but the problem is it's often impossible to tell ahead of time what will spread virally and what won't. Some of the most successful viral videos were never intended to spread virally, and some campaigns designed specifically to do so flop and never get anywhere. The key with viral videos is to make the video so entertaining or outrageous that viewers are driven to tell others about it, and the more people they tell, the faster and faster it spreads.

Viral videos also have their place and aren't the best option in all situations. For instance, viral videos generally work best for producing brand awareness. They generally aren't the best way to try and sell something. They work well as campaign drivers to get a product or service into the public's mind, but they're generally not going to product sales on their own. Instead, they need to be used in conjunction with other marketing techniques in order to produce the best results. The video can drive the awareness, but then you need to follow it up with marketing messages that are more sales oriented and will illicit more of a buying response.

From a cost perspective viral videos are a double edged sword. Companies with massive marketing budgets can spend huge amounts of money on their video campaigns in order to produce what they feel are videos with the best chance of spreading. However, if the video is based around a low cost concept, and that concept is strong enough, high levels of success can be obtained for very little money. The difference is that the big companies with the big budgets have the money to push their campaigns along if they aren't spreading as fast as they'd hoped. With a low cost video, the concept really has to be strong enough to carry the video on its own, which can be hard to do.

Business Making Bank With YouTube!

Will It Blend? is one of the most successful examples of a business using the power of video on the web to showcase and sell its products. In these videos, Tom Dickson, the founder of Blendtec showcases the power of his Blendtec blenders by pureeing various items.

But he doesn't just blend up anything. No, he makes his videos memorable by blending things like a golf club, an iPhone, toy cars, and more. These videos demonstrate Blendtec power and quality in a fun and memorable way that spreads virally, and Tom's videos have even spawned a huge number of parodies, all contributing to Blendtec's brand.

How could you creatively showcase your business in a way that would both engage and entertain viewers? Or better yet, do it so well that they want to show their friends?

Online Media Buying

If you think of the web as just another medium to advertise in, just like television, magazines, newspapers, etc, then there isn't any reason not to use some of the same advertising techniques that are available to you in offline media. This is completely true, and many of the same techniques and methods that companies apply in offline media translate over very well to the online world. Imagine the web as a giant stack of magazines on all different topics. Every website is its own self-contained magazine. Just like with print magazines, you can buy ad space to promote your company and its products or services. Just like with print media, the larger the readership, the more your ad will cost. The larger the ad, the more the ad will cost. The main difference is that with online media buying, you have more options as to how to use the ad space you buy.

For instance, in print media you're essentially limited to the confines of what you can print. Your reader can't interact with your ad in any way. Your ad can't have motion. It can't be dynamic. It has to be static text and images. When you move online, you can do just about anything in that ad space that the web allows. You can make your ad static, you can make it move, you can make it change colors, you can make it a video, you can make it an animation, you can make it a game, the possibilities are almost endless. Again, this is a great opportunity for you to try and engage your target audience on a higher level than you could with a simple print advertisement.

Keep in mind though that because most online ad buying is CPM, if your ad isn't well targeted and well written to ensure the reader wants to respond to it, you may end up spending a large chunk of money for little to no results at all. So if you are going to buy ad space on the net, you need to religiously test your ads, making sure that your copy is as persuasive as possible, and that you target your ad to only the groups that are responsive, and one of the groups that aren't.

Buying Ad Spots On Popular Websites

Here you see an ad spot that's been purchased on IGN.com, one of the internet's most popular websites for video game enthusiasts. In this case it's a rectangular banner placed prominently above the fold on the page.

Ads like this when targeted correctly can be very effective, but their cost needs to be analyzed carefully. The more popular the site the more expensive the ad, and overpaying for your ad can quickly sink its profitability.

Did this advertiser target his ad well? The ad is for a diet program. Diet programs generally tend to sell better to women, and the images in this ad are of a

Using Landing Pages

L anding pages are one of the most important types of webpage for any business looking to market themselves on the internet. Anytime you sell something online through any type of online direct response marketing, you should be using a landing page rather than sending your prospects to a generic page. The simple definition of a landing page is a specially designed, specific page that a prospect is sent to when they respond to a marketing campaign (whether that be clicking a link, entering their email address or typing in a URL). Whereas your company's normal website is where most of your general prospects, and ones who find you through organic search, will end up, a landing page is a special webpage you've put up specifically to give yourself the best chance of moving prospects from a specific campaign further through your sales funnel.

The reason landing pages are so important is that you simply can't afford to present your prospects with anything less than exactly what they're looking for, and a general page just isn't good enough for that. For instance if you're running a campaign to sell prospects a particular product, sending them to your company's general web page could be a big mistake. First of all, they might get there and be distracted by the navigation options, moving around or even leaving without actually ever getting to the information on the product you're trying to sell them. That's the worst case scenario. Alternately, they may end up buying another product. That isn't the worst thing in the world, but it will have a negative impact on the statistics for your campaign, and therefore your ability to tweak it.

So what goes into a good landing page then? Well, first and foremost, the obvious answer is good copy. Whether that means the text on the page or the script for your video, without good sales copy, you've got a seriously uphill battle in front of you as far as trying to get the prospect to take action goes. The fact is a great product with terrible copy will not sell, whereas a poor product with great copy will fly off the shelves. So your great product deserves great copy, and that is the single most important factor in the kind of success your landing page has. Well directed, specific, target copy, designed specifically to get the reader (or viewer) to take a distinct action come above all else. But it isn't the only thing.

Your landing page should also be (generally speaking) a lot simpler than the pages on your main website. The more there is going on within your landing page, the more there is to distract the reader from the offer you're presenting to them. This means that more often than not, in order to be as effective as possible, your landing page should be stripped down in comparison with your main website. That means no large or fancy header images, images should be well placed and carefully thought out, and most importantly *no navigation.*

Navigation can be and often is, the enemy of landing page effectiveness because it gives the user the option of *not* looking at the offer you've specifically directed them there to see. Sure, they can always just close the page, so really they always have that option, but by providing them with navigation like you have on your main website, you give them more ways to exercise that option! That's not what you want to do! For instance, if a person is genuinely interested in your company, they may not want to close your page. But if you give them navigation options, they may end up reading your "About Us" page or some recent press releases rather than reading the fantastic sales copy you worked so hard to put in front of them!

There is no excuse not to use a landing page for most of your promotions, and doing so will almost certainly have a positive impact on the amount of sales or conversions you get out of those campaigns, but like most things, if you do your landing pages poorly, they may end up hurting things rather than helping. After all, if your copy is no good, and you have no navigation, you've basically trapped your prospect on a page with no options to move on and nothing that makes them want to buy. What choice will they have but to close the page? But if you're doing your landing pages right, that won't even cross their minds. You won't distract them from your copy, and that copy will be so interesting and engaging, and make them so ready to take action on your offer that you won't need to worry about anything other than how to fill their order!

Using Landing Pages To Funnel Visitors

Rogers Video Direct landing page (top) vs. main page (bottom).

Affiliate Marketing

Imagine having an army of sales people working for you day and night, that you didn't have to keep on your payroll, didn't have to worry about scheduling, didn't have to provide office space to, and didn't have to worry about almost any of the expenses associated with having traditional employees? All you'd have to do is pay them their commission when they sell their product. Sound good? Sound like a great way to boost sales? Well, quite often, it is! It's called affiliate marketing and it's an absolutely massive market on the web. Countless business make use of affiliates to help drive their sales, from small businesses selling information products to giants like Amazon.

The reason affiliate marketing is so effective is that you're leveraging the efforts of a small army in order to help your business succeed.

Each affiliate is driven by the commission they're paid each time they sell your product, and if you offer a product that converts well, and a good commission, your affiliates will build up fast and that can mean huge sales numbers for your business. Essentially, affiliates are commission only sales people who work on the web and can sell your product 24 hours a day and from essentially anywhere.

A lot of people look at affiliate marketing and think of it as something that only works on a small time basis selling small time items, but this simply isn't true. While affiliate marketing does work extremely well on small ticket items, in reality, big ticket can (and do) succeed incredibly well with online affiliates. The reason is that big ticket items come with juicier commissions, and affiliates love higher commissions. For instance, if you're selling a $15 book, and you want to recruit affiliates, in order to entice them to promote your book, you'll probably need to give them at least a 50% commission, which is still only $7. This can eat into your profits *very* quickly. But if you're selling a $2000 product, and you give your affiliates only a 5% commission, they'll be making $100 per sale. That $100 is much more attractive than $7, and at only 5%, it won't have a huge effect on your margins.

It's also a good idea to provide your affiliates with materials to help make their jobs as online sales people easier. Remember that your affiliates will be promoting your products on the net, using mediums like blogs, articles, PPC and many of the same methods you would use to promote on your own. Since it's in your best interests for your affiliates to sell as much of your product as possible, you want to make it as easy as possible for them to do so. Providing an affiliate centre with graphical ads, email series, articles, PPC keywords and more that they can use in their efforts will be a big help in drawing in affiliates.

In order to use affiliates in your business you'll need a way to manage your program somehow. There are multiple ways to do that. Some larger businesses opt to have custom software built in order to track and manage their affiliates and affiliate payments, but for the average business, this is out of the question as the cost is extremely high. Luckily there are quite a few off the shelf solutions available. There are essentially two major choices when choosing how to run your affiliate program. You can use affiliate tracking software, which is software you install and use specifically to track your affiliate program, or you can choose to sell through one of the major affiliate networks, in which case the network takes care of all the tracking and management for you (for a cut of course).

Using affiliate tracking software gives you a certain amount of flexibility that might not exist with the affiliate network option. Things like setting your own terms of service, your own payment schedule, and changing certain options, are available to you with you if you use affiliate tracking software to manage your program, whereas when you use a network you're largely bound to their terms and their systems. The down side is that you take on an extra level of responsibility by managing your program completely on your own. You're responsible for *everything*.

By using an affiliate network, you may give up some options, but you also eliminate a lot of the headaches of running an affiliate program. You simply upload the information about your product and the network takes care of essentially everything else. When an affiliate makes a sale, the affiliate network takes care of the tracking and all of the payments. You're then sent your portion of the sale and the affiliate is sent theirs. The network also handles refunds and communications. For businesses selling physical, shippable goods, there are a few options. One is Amazon. Selling through Amazon gives you access to all the benefits that come with being attached to a company of that size and reputation. A *lot* of people go to Amazon to search for products, and Amazon has a *lot* of affiliates, who in turn become your affiliates! The other major option is Clickbank. For a long time Clickbank was only for digital products but they now allow shippable goods. Clickbank is one of the most popular affiliate marketplaces on the net, and a product that performs well on Clickbank will quickly be noticed and quickly amass an army of affiliates.

But before you dive in to affiliate marketing it's important for you to understand that while affiliate marketing is an incredibly good way to boost sales for a lot of businesses selling physical products, there are some dangers that you need to be careful of. When an affiliate makes a sale for you, while not directly under your employment, they're indirectly acting as an agent for your company. If that affiliate makes that sale based on illegal or misleading tactics, as well as the affiliate, your company could find itself in legal hot water. There have been documented incidents in the past of businesses getting into legal trouble based on the practices of affiliates, so it's important to make sure your affiliates are working on the up and up. This can be done by setting out very strict guidelines as to what is and is not allowed to be done under your affiliate program. It also helps to provide your affiliates with materials that coincide with your branding guidelines and that are legally sound. This reduces the chance of an affiliate accidentally doing something you'd rather they not do, or that they legally can't do.

If you utilize an affiliate network, the networks terms of service will lay down what is and isn't legally allowed, but it's still a good idea to check in on your affiliates every so often to make sure everything is on the straight and narrow (this is easily done if you're using a good web analytics package). If you use a piece of affiliate tracking software on your own, you'll be solely responsible for maintaining and enforcing the integrity of your affiliate program, and while only a very small number of affiliates will every do anything illegal or misleading, it's still nice to know that you've got the backup of a major affiliate network (even if from a legal standpoint it doesn't really protect you in the event of a rogue affiliate scamming consumers).

Another benefit to using a major affiliate network/store like Amazon or Clickbank is that they handle payment processing for you. This means that all of the payments done on your affiliates' sales are processed by the network. If you use Amazon, purchases are done through the Amazon shopping cart. If you use Clickbank, they have their own shopping cart system. Both are very secure and very reliable and highly trusted around the internet (particularly Amazon). This means if you don't have your own merchant account you can easily accept credit card payments on your products through the respective shopping carts of the affiliate networks. You can also do this with PayPal if you're managing your own affiliate program, but PayPal's fees can be hefty, and they offer no help with tracking or pay outs for your affiliates.

One of the major downsides of using certain affiliate marketing networks, specifically ones like Clickbank, is that when you make a sale, your profit from the sale doesn't go directly into your bank account or pocket. Instead it goes into your Clickbank account, and you're then paid out on a regular two week schedule. Once you're up and running, this normally isn't a problem, but it is worth it to note that payment to you is not immediate with many of these affiliate networks. If you aren't sure about affiliate marketing, your best bet is to put together a digital product like an e-book or report and sign up for Clickbank to test it out. You'll quickly get a feel for how the system works and it'll give you a chance to do some real world testing of the affiliate marketing system that has become so successful on the web. You can always remove your product from the marketplace and shut down your account at any time.

Digital Products

D igital products are a fantastic addition to any company's product line and can be used an a multitude of different ways to benefit the business. Now becoming more and more widely accepted across the net, digital products like e-books, reports and downloadable software are becoming more and more popular as an alternative to producing actual physical, shippable goods. Digital products offer many benefits over physical products, such as ease of production, low production costs and instant delivery. Low costs and quick delivery also make digital products attractive to consumers, who love a lower cost alternative and instant gratification. Digital products once suffered due to the bad stigma of being seen as a less than legitimate medium, but in the modern day, that stigma is gone and digital products are set to take off.

If you need proof that digital products are becoming more and more accepted, you need look no further than the huge trend in digitizing print books. New specially designed book reading platforms like the Kindle from Amazon and the Kobo, as well as functionality built into the next generation of tablet devices like the iPad, are driving an explosive expansion of the number of books available in digital format. For instance, in summer 2009 there were over 300,000 titles available for digital download including new releases, classics and books in all manners of niches. People are simply becoming more and more comfortable with the idea of interacting with lower cost digital versions of products they once bought in the physical world.

So what does this mean for your business? It means that it might be a great time for you to get in on the game and there are a number of ways you can do it, and a number of ways you can exploit this new trend to your benefit. A digital product gives you a powerful tool that you can use for any number of purposes in your marketing and sales. You might develop digital products specifically as new entries to your existing product line to sell to consumers. Or you might develop digital products to use as giveaways for existing or prospective customers, or to entice prospective customers to join your mailing list. You may use digital products as a way to gauge interest in certain niches and subject areas. The list goes on and on. Digital products are extremely versatile and their incredibly low production cost and ease of sale and delivery make them of benefit in many ways

The simplest type of digital product to create is an e-book, which is essentially just an electronic version of a standard book or report. On the simplest side, this could in theory be nothing more than a Microsoft Word file, which is how some early e-books were delivered. However, e-books in that lack professionalism and introduce certain problems. However, a professional quality e-book can be easily created by simply converting a document to a more secure, more standard file type such as a PDF file or one of the many other optional file types supported by e-book readers. The actual writing can easily be outsourced to a knowledgeable ghost writer if no one within the company is up to the task, and because the book is simply a file, there are zero printing costs.

Digital products tie in very closely with affiliate marketing, as the one of the largest affiliate networks/marketplaces, Clickbank, deals primarily in digital products of all types. Many affiliate marketers on the net are very comfortable (and very good), at selling digital products, and a good digital product with a good army of affiliates can bring in significant amounts of money. Some of the top selling products on Clickbank sell millions of copies a year representing tens and sometimes even hundreds of millions of dollars in revenues per year! While this is by far the exception rather than the rule, it illustrates the huge potential that exists for selling quality digital products online.

Software can also perform very well as a downloadable digital product but the cost of developing a useful piece of software are normally significantly higher than those associated with producing e-books and digital reports.

Whether you're developing your digital product for sale or for giveaway purposes, the question of what to base it on is often the first problem run into, and sometimes just thinking up the idea can take more time than the actual creation of the product. First of all, you'll want to create a product that relates to your core business. If you own a garden centre, a digital product on growing vegetables at home will probably be of more benefit to growing your business than one about car repair. Once you see the power of selling digital products online it can become tempting to produce more and more in all subject fields, but it's important to remember that you're using these digital products as a tool to grow your business, and not making them into your business itself (although a lot of people make very good incomes off of nothing but digital product creation).

The key is to treat the digital product just like you would any of your physical products. Your customers need something, and you're going to give it to them. With digital products, you're selling information, so ask yourself what kinds of problems your customers have that you have the solutions to, and can put onto paper. These are the kinds of topics that make great information products. Once you've got your topic you can then decide what you'd like to do with your product. This is important because products you'll sell and products you'll give away need to be written differently. First of all, giveaway products are almost always significantly shorter than ones that go up for sake. If you're selling someone an e-book for $37, you'll need it to be more substantial than one you're giving away in exchange for an email address, which could be as short as one or two pages!

Another important distinction is that if you're going to be giving the product away, then you might not want to give *too much* away. Think about it, if you're trying to sell someone your widget installation services, and you give them a free guide on DIY widget installation, you may have just mad yourself unnecessary! While the odds are you won't find yourself in the spot of making your own business obsolete with your new digital product, the point is that you need to consider its purpose in order to know how much information to give away. Do you want the reader to contact you for more information? Do you want the reader to go to your website and make a purchase? Do you want the reader to switch to you from a competitor? There are a lot of things you can do with giveaway information products, and you need to tailor your efforts to match the goal.

Google Television Ads

Television advertising has long been seen as the realm of large corporations. It's so expensive to produce a commercial, and then so much more expensive to buy airtime for it, that most small and medium sized businesses didn't have a prayer. Sure you might be able to get a brief spot on a local public access channel, but advertising on cable was out of the question. Who would imagine that one day businesses would be able to book commercial airtime spots on most major cable networks from the comfort of their own home or office? With the new television ads service from Google, that's now possible. Google AdWords TV Ads allows users to upload their commercials in accepted video formats and then book airtime for those commercials on their choice of many of the biggest and most popular networks and cable channels.

Creating your television ad is up to you and you have some options If you're confident in your own abilities to produce a quality video you can shoot and upload your own ad spot. Google TV ads accept multiple standard video file formats including MPEG2 and AVI. However, making video that looks professional is hard, so you might want to leave it to the actual professionals! If that's the case, Google offers an ad creation marketplace where you can choose from a large selection of different video production firms and see general quotes on what different types of videos will cost. On the low end you may be able to get a simple commercial for as little as $300. However some of the examples also run as high as $60,000! It really depends on what you need! Finally, Google advertisers have access to SpotMixer, which is an online ad development tool that gives the user the ability to quickly mix text, stock footage and royalty free audio and video to put together ads.

Everything is set up right through your AdWords account and much like traditional AdWords you get near real time feedback on your campaigns including airings, your ad's reach (market size), frequency (how often your ad has been seen)., played spots, impressions, average viewing time, CPM and more. You can also use some of Google's other tools like Google's toll free number service to add more layers to your metrics. However, in order to get the most information on how your campaign is converting you'll need to add your own conversion tracking into the ad. The easiest way to do this is to include a unique URL or phone number in the ad so you can track which leads are coming directly from that campaign. Google's toll free number service offers call tracking if used in conjunction with Google TV ads.

The system works much the same way AdWords does in that it's based on a bidding system. You set a maximum bid on what you want to pay per thousand impressions, and your ad will air based on that. You then set a daily budget which Google will adhere to when airing your ad, select the networks and time slots you want to show on, target your audience, and you're ready to go. What running your ads will cost you depends entirely on where and when you want them shown. Airing your ad on a major network like Fox during prime time hours will require a very large bid, whereas airing on a much smaller niche network, or very late at night, will significantly lower your bid. In fact, you can run a single ad spot for as low as $20! The really important thing is in your targeting, because often times, you simply don't *need* to run your spots during the peak times that require a mint in funding. If you do your targeting properly, and set your ad to air during times that won't break the bank but also give you the exposure you require, you can end up with a successful TV campaign at a very affordable price!

Section Four:

Staying Connected

The Importance of Staying Connected

New customers are always great, but as most business owners know, your most valuable customers are normally your existing customers. If you're in a business where customers make repeat purchases, then it is a huge mistake to take those existing customers for granted and simply assume that they'll come back to you when they need something. The costs associated with finding a new customer are significantly higher than the cost associated with maintaining an existing customer, so you need to be sure that you're constantly doing your best to retain your current client base. This concept of the importance of repeat business can sometimes become clouded behind the sometimes blinding drive to increase current sales levels, but it's extremely important to think of your customers in the long term as well as just the short term.

'Lifetime value of a customer' (LVC) is likely a term you're familiar with. Essentially just because a customer spends $1000 with you today doesn't mean that the value of that customer is worth $1000. Instead you have to take into account the value of that customer across the entire lifetime of their purchases with you. A customer who only buys $1000 of goods and services from you once and then never again *is* worth $1000, but what if they come back 10 more times? They're worth *a lot* more. We won't get into the actual calculations about LVC because that isn't what this section is about (if you're curious it involves the present value of a customer's future purchases). What this section is about is how to acknowledge that importance and make sure you're keeping your customers around for as long as possible!

So how do you make sure your customers keep coming back? Well the quick and obvious answer is great customer service. Unfortunately though a lot of companies think customer service means responding to complaints and problems, but in reality, it's much more than that. One of the most important, and often most ignored, aspects of great customer service is *staying connected*. By staying connected we mean keeping a continuous point of contact between you and your existing customers. This doesn't revolve around problems, in fact it doesn't really have to revolve around anything. All that's important is that you keep a constant line open between you and the people who buy from you. Do this and your business will benefit greatly as a result.

The reason is that as soon as you cease to communicate with your customers they begin to forget about you. If they don't hear from you, what happens is that you essentially just become another business in the Yellow Pages. When it comes time for them to replace their widget, they may come back to you, or they may go somewhere else. And the longer the gap between purchases, the more and more your odds decrease. What you want is to destroy that trend. You want to make sure that your customers are consistently thinking about your business. That way, when it comes time to make another purchase, you'll immediately come to mind. The way to do this is by staying constantly connected with your customers. A consumer knows they can trust a company that takes the time to stay in contact with them, and trust is the key.

How you choose to stay in contact with them is up to you, and there are a million options. A card on their birthday, an exclusive coupon in their email, a newsletter, amusing blog posts, all these things are great options. The medium isn't as important as the message though, and on the surface that message might be 'happy birthday', but deeper down the message is 'we value you as a customer and we value communicating with you'. Send that message and your business will boom.

One of the most important aspects of staying connected is the extra value that it provides for your customers. This value isn't necessarily related to an existing purchase, but is more added value in the relationship in general. Just the act of communicating alone can add this extra value, but aside from that there are certain things you can do to help add value to your communications. Things like coupons, special information, special offers, even just updates on what's going on with your business or in your community are all value adding things. The important part is to make sure that your communications with your customer are providing them with something beneficial and the more you can provide them with the more eager they'll be to keep in communication with you.

Using Social Media

S ocial media is all about connecting people on the internet, and while initially that was limited mostly to people connecting with other people outside the business world, many of the most forward thinking businesses quickly realized the potential that social media had to be used for business purposes. Social media is one the customer-centric company's best friends because social media makes it incredibly easy to provide your customers with a constant (literally) and non-intrusive way to stay in contact with your business. Not to mention that the cost of using social media to stay in contact with your customers is extremely low. So why wouldn't you make use of an effective, low cost method of communicating with your customers in ways that they enjoy being communicated with? Social media is a perfect way for you to connect with your customers.

Facebook

Facebook is one of the world's more popular websites and by far the most popular social network on the web. Facebook started out when college students wanted a way to connect with their fellow students and decided to build just such a place on the web. Years later it's now worth multiple billions of dollars and boasts over 400 million active users. A lot of people think of Facebook as being something student's use, but that couldn't be farther from the truth. Facebook has users of all ages, and many of the world's biggest corporations have active Facebook groups and users, including Google, IBM, and more. You'd be surprised how many of your customers might be on Facebook (so why not ask?)

Businesses aren't supposed to use personal profiles on Facebook, although some do, but officially, businesses are supposed to open a business account which has different functionality from a personal account. Your business account will allow you to create Facebook pages, which are slightly different than profiles. Through your Facebook pages you can promote and inform on your products, make special offers to your Facebook subscribers and more. You can also share articles, useful links, blog posts, or anything else you find on the net that you think would be of benefit to your customers. On the personal side of things, while you can't technically use Facebook for your business, you and your employees can use your personal

Facebook profiles to update your friend groups on business related notes. You while your business technically can't have its own personal profile, if you want to, you can get around that by adding customers to your personal profile updating that personal profile with communications relevant to your business.

One word of warning though is that because Facebook is such a personal form of social networking, if you do decide to use your personal profile to help promote your business, you need to be careful with how you manage your profile and contacts. People normally add their families and friends on Facebook, and if you're using your personal profile you're no different. However, this means that unless you take steps to prevent it your business contacts and customers will also have access to all of the information all of those people post on your profile. Do you really want business contacts or customers seeing those embarrassing pictures from the Christmas party that someone posts? No way. Luckily, you can place your contacts in different groups and specify how much access each group has to your information. So you can add all your business contacts and customers into a group that only has access to the parts of your profile you want them to.

Twitter

Twitter is one of the most innovative, easiest to use social media sites on the internet, but also one of the most perplexing. Founded as a type of "mini-blogging" platform, Twitter has become one of the most popular, most used websites on the net, but yet the site itself has no business model and no real way of producing revenues, which leads many analysts to wonder what its future will be. But regardless of its future, the fact is that right now, Twitter is one of the hottest things on the internet, and it's so easy to get started with that your business absolutely can't afford not to have a Twitter account.

The basic premise of Twitter is that each post or "tweet" can be no longer than 140 characters, so everything on Twitter is short and to the point. Much like Facebook you add or "follow" people. When you follow someone, their tweets come up on your home page. When someone follows you, your tweets come up on their homepage. There are other functionalities built in like private messages, but the tweet is the backbone of twitter and the real power of Twitter for business lies in the tweet. The reason is the tweet is how you'll communicate with your customers (both existing and potential). When your customers follow you on Twitter, anytime you post a tweet it shows up on their home page for them to read along with all of the tweets from the other accounts they're following. This is a simple and effective way of letting customers know what's going on, and to share links to special promotions, blog posts, and more. But the tweet has one secret weapon that is even more powerful.

The re-tweet is much like the tweet except that a re-tweet is someone passing on what you've tweeted. So for instance, if you write a tweet and one of your customers that follows you likes it, they can then re-tweet that on their own Twitter feed and it'll then also show up to *everyone that follows them*! Do you see the amazing power here? Re-tweets are one of the most powerful things on the internet bar none, and if one of your tweets gets noticed and starts being re-tweeted, your list of followers will explode, and the offer or message you placed in that original tweet will grow wings and spread like wildfire. Imagine the potential in that?

If you have 100 followers on Twitter, and each of those people have 10 followers, if you could get each of them to re-tweet something you post, instead of being seen by only 100 people, it would be seen by 1000 people! And if the 900 extra people you reached also re-tweet your post, the numbers just keep going up and up! No imagine that your original tweet was a promotional one announcing a new sale or special offer. The business that the single tweet you posted has the potential to generate is almost mind-numbing. This isn't rocket science, in fact it's simple, and many businesses have harnessed the power of the tweet and re-tweet to not only keep in contact with their customers, but to boost their sales!

Twitter is also a great place for executives and employees to post personally about topics relating to your business. Some of the world's most famous entrepreneurs and executives have personal twitter accounts that they use to communicate with followers about personal matters and business matters alike. If guys like Richard Branson and Bill Gates can find a reason to get on Twitter, then surely there must be some merit to it! It's also a great way to keep tabs on what people are saying about you, and some businesses actually respond faster to tweets directed at them than they do to help desk inquiries!

LinkedIn

LinkedIn is a social network that focuses on connecting professionals, employers, employees and all manners of business people into multiple level networks. One of the most interesting features of LinkedIn is that it allows you to get an accurate view of how wide your network reaches up to three degrees of separation. So when you add a contact on LinkedIn, you're able to also see who your contact's contacts are, and so forth. Because it's a business related site, there isn't a lot of value for businesses in LinkedIn for consumer level communications. However, for business to business dealings LinkedIn is one of the most productive places a company can be in the world of social media.

If you're a company that does B2B sales, LinkedIn is the place for you. All you have to do is search for your existing business contacts on LinkedIn either by email address or by name. Any of your contacts that you find are then just a click away from being added to your profile. Once you're connected you can make and receive recommendations, ask to be connected to contacts further down the tree and send messages back and forth among the contacts on your profile. You have a "status" much like Facebook which you can use to update your contacts as to your current activities, and it is in no way uncommon for employers to find employees through LinkedIn, or for companies to find vendors through LinkedIn contacts. LinkedIn also allows users to join groups with like minded individuals where discussions can be had, meetings set up and more. These groups also come with the power of email marketing, because the group "owner" can broadcast messages to all of the group members. This means that if you can create a group and persuade people in your existing client base or potential client base to join, you have one more avenue of communication open to you than you would otherwise.

Social Media Mistakes

There are some common misconceptions about social media and one of them is that you can just set your accounts up and forget them and they'll continue to be of any use to you. This is simply untrue. The entire point of social media and social networking is interaction. It's what all the major platforms are built for, and it's the only thing that people use them for. So if you don't plan to interact, then you're wasting your time. You simply can't just set up an account and expect it to have any sort of effectiveness. You need to keep up to speed with updating your accounts or people will forget about them or stop following them.

Another big mistake with social media is crossing over that fine line from productivity into wasting time. Social media can be very addicting, even when using it for business, and this is especially true if you mix your business with your personal accounts. You may find yourself rationalizing spending time on Facebook or Twitter because it's good for business when in reality you're just clicking around without actually doing anything productive. This is a real danger online, especially with social media. So you need to make sure that when you or your employees begin incorporating social media into your daily business routine, that it's done in moderation and only in productive a productive manner!

Big Players Recognizing The Value Of Facebook

Nestle is the world's largest food and nutrition company, and their brand name is known and respected around the world. Yet even with that incredible brand strength Nestle understands the value of keeping in contact with their customers.

Their Facebook group, pictured above, has over 100,000 followers, a number that is sure to grow astronomically as the page ages. They use the page to make announcements about new products and brands, new humanitarian initiatives, company news, and for general communication with their customers.

Business Blogging

Blogs are the new king of the web. They offer fresh, up to date content for the millions and millions of users on the web to gobble up. They offer opinions, reviews, fiction, news updates, and more. But they also do business, and they do business really, really well. Blogs are quickly becoming one of the most popular and most effective ways that companies all over the world are using to reach out to their customers to offer a new line of communication. Not to mention that having a business blog can have a lot of side benefits for your overall web marketing efforts. The fact is that there isn't really any way in which a blog isn't good for your business. Blogs are great for SEO, they're great for technical support and customer service, and most importantly, they're great for staying connected!

Users love blogs for the same reason that Google loves blogs; fresh content. Fresh content is what makes Google favor blog platforms so heavily in its rankings and fresh content is what keeps people coming back to blogs over and over again, and that's the key, is return traffic! A website for your business is a necessity because it gives people a place to find your business online, but it's not exactly a personal connection that goes on between a potential or existing customer and a company's main website. However, a blog breaks that down. A blog *is* a personal connection because it isn't just an online brochure or a set of information, it's a *discussion*. Blogs are so powerful because unlike standard website, they don't just broadcast in one direction, but instead they let readers have their own say as well, and that discussion is what builds community, and that's exactly what you want your customers to feel like they're a part of.

Unlike Facebook and Twitter, blogs allow you to communicate in some serious detail. Facebook and Twitter both lend themselves to shorter, briefer messages, but on your blog you can write at length. If it takes you 1000 words to get your point across, so be it (but try not to bore your readers!) This means that while Facebook and Twitter are great for quick updates, your blog gives you a chance to really give your customers some great information. Whether it be informative articles on topics they're interested relating to your business, or detailed explanations of upcoming events, sales, problems, or anything else of value.

If you consider your company's main website as the face of your business on the web, then think of your blog as your company's personality. Your main website is there to exude the professionalism and integrity of your business. Your blog is there to present the personal, more human side of your business, and customers love doing business with a company that is more than just a logo and slogan. The more personal your business seems, the more loyalty your customers will feel. We've all been frustrated before by automated messages on phone calls and impersonal form emails. We all know that we prefer doing business with companies that make us feel like we're important and not just another number in line. A blog is a great way to do that.

The key is to regularly update your blog with up to date information on all the different things you can provide that will interest your readers, and then to respond to their reactions. That second part is something worth saying again. You need to *respond*. Don't treat your blog as a broadcast. It's not something you send to them and they ingest. It's a give and take. When you put up a blog post, your customers will, ideally, comment on it with their own thoughts or questions on the subject. If you just let those comments sit there, your customers will feel ignored and the blog will have lost some of its power. But if you respond, you've taken a huge step in your relationship with that customer because you've opened a dialogue. They're not on the phone pressing zero and hoping for an operator, they're getting a real response from a real person.

Another question relating to the personal element that a blog provides is whether to blog as the business or blog as an individual? This is an important distinction and there are many examples of both. Some companies blog under the company name and some companies blog as individuals, often with the CEO or a high ranking executive representing the online face of the blog. The best way to do it is actually to do it both ways! That is, don't choose one or the other, but have multiple blogs representing different parts of the company. For instance, many online businesses are now opting to have a technical support blog that allows the company to update customers on any service interruptions, updates or problems that may be on the horizon. Then they'll also have a blog for the business itself which might be written by an individual employee. Many businesses even encourage *all* of their employees to get online and maintain a blog. There really isn't a limit as to the number of people within your organization that can be blogging. The more the merrier as they say!

Your options for the actual technical side of your blog are many. There are plenty of online, hosted blogging services that you can use free of charge. However they're free for a reason. The features can be limited, the designs are often less than appealing, and most importantly, you're bound by someone else's terms of service, and they can axe your blog at any time they feel and there is absolutely nothing you can do about it. The other option is an installed platform, such as Wordpress, which you host yourself and install under your

own domain name. The options you have with these kinds of solutions are generally much wider than what you get from the free online options, and a lot of very successful companies use these types of systems, called content management systems (CMS), for their blogging needs. Finally, you can have a custom build blog and CMS back end built for you. The advantage to this is that it's highly secure, but the downside is that it's extremely costly and out of the budget of most small and medium businesses.

Much like the social media sites mentioned in the previous section, consistency is important in blogging. A blog that goes without being updated is a blog that quickly dies. You need to keep posting regularly for your blog to be at its most effective. Your customers need to know that if they go back to your blog every so many days, that there will be a new post there waiting for them to read. Don't worry though because posting to your blog doesn't have to take long. It can be something you do in 10 or 15 minutes and it doesn't even have to be every single day. But you do have to keep with it. A nice upside to that consistency though is that the more you post to your blog, the more of your posts will get indexed in the search engine, and the more likely it is that potential clients will find your company on their own using search engines!

Forum Participation

Communities are one of the biggest parts of the online experience, and millions of internet users spend hours each day visiting online forums. Forums and message boards are one of the biggest draws on the net, and some of the largest forums have hundreds of thousands of active users and millions of posts. The members there may never have met each other in the real world and may even be on opposite sides of the Earth from each other, but yet they have a relationship and often consider themselves friends. Some forums even have meet ups where some members will drive for hours or even hop on flights to be there. The fact of the matter is, internet communities are often (very often) more active than actual real world communities, and this incredible level of interaction means you have an opportunity to get in on the game and make a name for yourself.

There may or may not be forums out there made up of your customer base, but there is a very good chance that there are. And the more widespread your customer base is, the higher the likelihood. If you're an exclusively local seller, then you may find yourself in a tough spot for finding communities online to tap into. However if you're a national seller, then the chances are very high that a decent sized chunk of your customer base are hanging out together somewhere online. And if they are, you're making a *huge* mistake by not participating yourself. The benefits of doing so (and consequences of not) are so significant that you'd be crazy not to get into the mix.

First let's talk briefly about the consequences. A fact of life in the current digital world is that just because you aren't on the internet doesn't mean that people there aren't talking about you! Add to that the commonly understood fact that when it comes to word of mouth, bad reviews are far more detrimental for your business than good reviews are beneficial. So what that essentially means is that if you've got a relatively large customer base, then someone, somewhere is probably griping about you. You could be the best company on earth, but someone, somewhere, has had a bad experience. If that someone finds their way into a group of other customers or potential customers, you could have some trouble! By not actively monitoring and participating in any online discussion groups with your customer base (existing or potential) involved, you're basically giving yourself no line of defense. Simply by being present to help with problems that may come up you'll not only curb any bad reviews before they really get started, and also build yourself a reputation as a business that cares about its customers and actively seeks to help them.

The benefits are equally as powerful. By being a regular contributor to the online communities where your customer base spends time, you build a level of trust that it can be incredibly difficult to build elsewhere. A company that spends time conversing with its customers on a casual basis and taking care of any complaints that comes up is a company that develops a bond with those customers. When it comes time to make a purchase, a customer can either choose to go with a faceless company they may have seen in an ad somewhere, or they can choose to go with a company they have direct experience, that they know is there to help, and they feel is part of their community. Who are they going to choose? It's an easy choice. By participating in their online social groups, you stick your brand in your customers' brains and you ensure that when purchase time comes, that you're the first business they think of.

There is a fine line you have to walk though when it comes to forum participation. Done right it's of huge value to your business, but done wrong, it can actually be incredibly harmful to your business. The reason is that when you participate in online communities, if it appears that you're there for promotional reasons, they'll reject you and your business, and the mark it leaves on your reputation can be irreparable among those people. Not to mention that it's against most message boards' terms of service for companies to make accounts for promotional purposes (that's called advertising and they want you to pay them!) Your participation has to be natural and actually add to the conversation. Make use of your specialized knowledge and expert status to help the members of the community without pitching them your services. Be there to answer questions and help with problems, and even participate in some of the off-topic random banter that goes on. Always make sure to be conscious of your image and how you're presenting yourself, and always remember that in the end you want to make as many of these people customers as possible, but make sure you don't come off as a salesman. If you do, they'll feel like you're intruding and you'll only end up doing yourself more harm than good.

Selling Goalie Equipment One Post At A Time

Battram Custom Goal Equipment is a fantastic example of a small business that used forum participation as a main driver to build its brand. Battram's owner, Scott Battram of Curries, Ontario, built a name for himself, and his brand, by participating on one of the largest online forums for ice hockey goalies.

But Scott didn't just hit the net to hock his wares. Far from it. Scott found success by becoming one of the most respected members of the online community by providing valuable insight and adding positively to discussions.

Once he'd established his name and reputation among the large group of potential customers, they were glad to try out his products, and from there the quality of his products and customer service did the talking for themselves.

Mailing Lists and Auto Responders

If your customers told you that they wanted to be contacted specifically by you so that they could be updated on news, valuable information, specials, coupons and more, would you do it? Of course you would! And what if doing so was one of the most cost effective ways of marketing available to you? You'd have no reason not to. Welcome to the online mailing list. Imagine if your business had a mailing list of 10,000 physical addresses of customers and potential customers who'd requested to be sent your newsletter. What would the costs of mailing to that list be like? Well for one thing you're probably looking at a few thousand dollars minimum for postage alone each time you send out a single mailer in a standard envelope. Not to mention printing, the time involved, etc. How often could you send one out? Once a month? How often would you *like* to send one out?

Online mailing lists take all the benefits of a physical newsletter and supercharge them. You still get the relationship building contact. You still get the ability to update your customers on a regular basis. You still get the promotional benefits. But the cost is so much lower, and the production process so much simpler that you can now make those contacts far more often, at a far lower cost. Take that same 10,000 person list. Now you have no printing costs. Your distribution is as simple as the click of a button. No envelopes needed, no postage needed, nothing. All you pay is your monthly fee for your auto responder package which is *significantly* less than the cost of even a single mailing to your physical mailing list.

Now instead of sending out your newsletter once every month or even once every two months, you can send it out once every week, or twice every week. The amount of extra contact that you can have with your existing and potential customers using an online mailing list and an auto responder is so much higher than you can with a physical mailing list and paper mailers that you can build a much stronger relationship with your customers. However that only works if you're providing them with useful information on a regular basis. Remember, you don't want to come off as a salesman, and if the members of your mailing list feel like all you do is sell to them, they'll unsubscribe and you'll lose them not only as readers but likely as customers as well. The key is to provide useful, beneficial content to your subscribers, and then trickle your promotions in among them.

Studies have shown that it can take up to seven or more contacts with a prospect before they're ready to buy. Using a standard mailing list that could take you a year! But with an online mailing list, you could make that prospect into a customer in a matter of weeks. But again, if you come off as pushy, you'll have the opposite effect! A good rule is to send out promotions at a rate of no more than once for every two non-promotional messages you send out. Also keep in mind we're talking purely promotional messages. Things like valuable coupons or free offers are normally more than welcome from readers, and it's completely safe to send out a coupon or special deal offer in each of your mailings.

The beauty of these kinds of lists is that they're made up of people who have opted-in to your list (normally even requiring a double opt-in) and therefore you're marketing to people who know are interested in you, your business or its services, because they've confirmed so when they signed up to be on your mailing list. You can now be sure you're spending your time working towards building relationships (ideally of the purchasing kind) with people who have proven themselves to be receptive. Even if they never read your emails, the fact that they see you in their inbox on a regular basis and remember that they asked for that information works in your favor because you're delivering on something they asked for, even if they never get around to using it.

The actual task of list building is one of your prime challenges with mailing lists and auto-responders. You want to have as big a list of qualified prospects as possible, but the bigger your list the harder and more expensive it becomes to manage, so you want to make sure you *only* have prospects and not people who aren't ever going to even consider making a purchase. So how do you go about making sure you get every qualified prospect possible and leave out all the rest? First you determine who is a qualified prospect for your list. This is going to determine how you capture your leads. One of the simplest ways is geography. If you're a nation-wide seller, then you don't have much to worry about geographically. But if you're a local seller, then having someone across the country on your list doesn't provide you with a potential customer, but does contribute to your costs. Do you only want to market to existing customers? Do you want to market to potential customers? Both?

Once you've defined who you consider a qualified prospect you can begin capturing leads. The first and most obvious place to capture email addresses is your website. If you're looking nationally or internationally, then feel free to capture leads on your main website. If you're regional or local, you'll want to use special landing pages that you only advertise to people in your target area. That way your list will be purely qualified prospects. You have a lot of options as to how to collect from your web pages. You can use light boxes, inline forms, pop-ups, pop-unders, etc. You'll want to test to find out what produces the best for your site (remember; test, test, test!) Aside from your website and landing pages, you should be looking to collect emails in just about any other place you can (as long as it fits in with your predefined qualifications). Create a landing page with the sole purpose of collecting emails for your list and print the links on all of your paper materials. Print it in your paper newsletter, print it on your receipts, print it anywhere you feel will help you grab more email addresses. More email addresses means more leads.

If you're marketing to more than one group it's very important that you segment your list. For instance, if you plan to market to existing customers and potential customers, it's very important that you have them on separate mailing lists. You can re-use your non-promotional messages for both, but when it comes time to send promotional messages, you need these two groups separated to ensure you aren't pushing the same products or services on people who've already purchased them! This can be done by simply setting up one list to feed the other. If a member of your prospect list makes a purchase, they're automatically moved to (or prompted to join) your customer list. This adds them to the customer list and removes them from the prospect list. Simple things like this can have a massive impact on the effectiveness of your mailing lists so it's important not to ignore them.

Conclusion:

H opefully you've now got a much deeper understanding of what the different options are for your business in the field of internet marketing. The internet is a relatively new and very exciting way for businesses to reach out to customers, and at this point hopefully you're very excited about getting some new digital systems up and running for your business. The important thing to remember is that *any* business can benefit from implementing digital systems and using the internet in their marketing efforts. There is no business and no industry that is immune to the benefits of marketing on the web. The key is to analyze your business, your current systems, marketing efforts, customers, products and every other aspect in order to judge what types of digital marketing are right for you, and in what capacity.

It's easy for business owners to simply subscribe to the old saying "if it ain't broke, don't fix it", and in a sense this is good advice, but it could also be costly. Just because your business is already doing alright, or succeeding, doesn't mean it couldn't be doing better. You very well could be spending less money, saving time, and earning more. But the first thing you need to do is decide that you're ready to embrace the modern era of digital marketing technology and methodology. Once you do that, you'll be well on your way to bringing your business into synch with today's modern marketing methods, and those to come in the future!

Good luck with your future business and marketing endeavors, and may they make great use of the amazing new digital methods now available to us all!

www.ingramcontent.com/pod-product-compliance
Lightning Source LLC
Chambersburg PA
CBHW032016170526
45157CB00002B/719